CW00557030

ACCESSIBILITY AND INCLUSION OF PEOPLE WITH DISABILITIES IN U.S. FOREIGN ASSISTANCE PROGRAMS

DISABILITY AND THE DISABLED-ISSUES, LAWS AND PROGRAMS

Additional books in this series can be found on Nova's website under the Series tab.

Additional E-books in this series can be found on Nova's website under the E-book tab.

ACCESSIBILITY AND INCLUSION OF PEOPLE WITH DISABILITIES IN U.S. FOREIGN ASSISTANCE PROGRAMS

TRISTON W. PRUETT
EDITOR

publishers
New York

Library of Congress Cataloging-in-Publication Data

ISBN: 978-1-62808-324-8

Published by Nova Science Publishers, Inc. † New York

CONTENTS

PREFACE

This book's aim is to advance understanding and to promote accessibility and inclusion of people with disabilities in foreign assistance programs funded by the United States. This book reviews U.S. federal disability laws, the United States Agency for International Development's (USAID) Disability Policy, and the Convention on the Rights of Persons with Disabilities (CRPD) and discusses their application to U.S. foreign assistance programs. More than one billion people, 15 percent of the world's population, have a disability. The number continues to grow as a result of aging populations, poverty, armed conflict, and AIDs. Postconflict and developing countries have a significant proportion of people with disabilities. Although people with disabilities make up a large segment of the population in many countries, they continue to face horrific forms of discrimination and segregation throughout the world. This book examines the work of USAID, the U.S. Department of State (DOS), and the U.S. Department of Defense (DOD), and provides recommendations that will strengthen the operation of these agencies by ensuring U.S. Government funding is used in a manner that is accessible to and inclusive of people with disabilities.

Chapter 1 – The overarching aim of this report is to advance understanding and to promote accessibility and inclusion of people with disabilities in foreign assistance programs funded by the United States. The report reviews U.S. federal disability laws, the United States Agency for International Development's (USAID) Disability Policy, and the Convention on the Rights of Persons with Disabilities (CRPD) and discusses their application to U.S. foreign assistance programs. The report examines the work of USAID, the U.S. Department of State (DOS), and the U.S. Department of Defense (DOD), and provides recommendations that will strengthen the operation of these agencies by ensuring U.S. Government funding is used in a manner that is accessible to and inclusive of people with disabilities.

More than one billion people, 15 percent of the world's population, have a disability. The number continues to grow as a result of aging populations, poverty, armed conflict, and AIDS. Postconflict and developing countries have a significant proportion of people with disabilities. Although people with disabilities make up a large segment of the population in many countries, they continue to face horrific forms of discrimination and segregation throughout the world.

The United States has been a leader in advancing the rights of people with disabilities and must continue to promote disability rights through its international development work. The United States invests billions of taxpayer dollars each year into foreign assistance programs that foster international diplomacy and development. Notably, these programs develop economies, promote democracy and governance, provide humanitarian assistance, build new infrastructure, and advance and protect human rights. The United States cannot effectively accomplish the goals of foreign assistance programs unless it undertakes measures to ensure that the programs are accessible to and inclusive of people with disabilities.

To ensure effective and sustainable economic development and poverty eradication, people with disabilities must benefit from economic development programs. Micro-level interventions aimed at income generation and macro-level interventions designed to create legal and regulatory frameworks must be accessible to people with disabilities.

Chapter 2 – The U.S. Agency for International Development (USAID) is committed to the inclusion of people who have physical and cognitive disabilities and those who advocate and offer services on behalf of people with disabilities. This commitment extends from the design and implementation of USAID programming to advocacy for and outreach to people with disabilities. USAID's policy on disability is as follows: To avoid discrimination against people with disabilities in programs which USAID funds and to stimulate an engagement of host country counterparts, governments, implementing organizations and other donors in promoting a climate of nondiscrimination against and equal opportunity for people with disabilities. The USAID policy on disability is to promote the inclusion of people with disabilities both within USAID programs and in host countries where USAID has programs.

For purposes of this policy, a disability is defined as a physical or cognitive impairment that affects a major life function, consistent with the definition of the Rehabilitation Act.

USAID commitment to disability issues is not new. A 1996 report ("Activities Addressing the Needs of Person with Disabilities," USAID document PN−ABY−746) described the many and varied Agency−sponsored activities in provisioning of prosthetics, treatment and prevention of blindness and special education, providing medical training of individuals who assist persons with disabilities, building advocacy and management capabilities of local organizations that represent the disabled, and the like. This policy is designed to build upon current activities and to enhance the effectiveness of the Agency's commitment.

The policy applies to Agency program funds only, and complements existing USAID disability policies which relate to staffing and personnel procedures. One of the best means of raising awareness in programs is to actively pursue those personnel procedures so that Agency staffing patterns reflect the intention of Agency programs.

The Americans with Disabilities Act of 1990 (ADA) is generally not applicable to USAID's overseas programs. While the ADA applies to U.S. citizens (including USAID employees) overseas, it does not apply to non−U.S. citizens, who are the primary beneficiaries of USAID programs. The USAID disability policy is thus in part an effort to extend the spirit of the ADA in areas beyond the jurisdiction of U.S. law.

In: Accessibility and Inclusion of People ...   ISBN: 978-1-62808-324-8
Editor: Triston W. Pruett   © 2013 Nova Science Publishers, Inc.

Chapter 1

TOWARD THE FULL INCLUSION OF PEOPLE WITH DISABILITIES: EXAMINING THE ACCESSIBILITY OF OVERSEAS FACILITIES AND PROGRAMS FUNDED BY THE UNITED STATES NATIONAL COUNCIL ON DISABILITY[*]

National Council on Disability

LETTER OF TRANSMITTAL

The President
The White House
Washington, DC 20500

Dear Mr. President:

The National Council on Disability is pleased to submit the enclosed report "Toward the Full Inclusion of People with Disabilities: Examining the

---

[*] This report was released by the National Council on Disability, February 2013.

Accessibility of Overseas Facilities and Programs Funded by the United States."

More than one billion people, 15 percent of the world's population, have a disability. The prevalence of disability continues to grow due to aging, poverty, armed conflict, and AIDS, among other contributing factors. Post-conflict and developing countries have a significant proportion of people with disabilities as a result. Although people with disabilities make up a large segment of the population in many countries, they continue to face intolerable forms of discrimination and segregation throughout the world.

The United States invests billions of taxpayer dollars each year into foreign assistance programs that foster international diplomacy and development, aimed at improving the quality of life for people around the world. These programs develop economies, promote democracy and governance, provide humanitarian assistance, build new infrastructure, and advance and protect human rights. Given that 15 percent of the world population is made up of people with disabilities, and growing, the United States cannot effectively accomplish the goals of foreign assistance programs unless it undertakes measures to ensure that the programs are accessible to and inclusive of people with disabilities.

NCD undertook this study to advance understanding and to promote accessibility and inclusion of people with disabilities in foreign assistance programs funded by the United States. The report reviews U.S. federal disability laws, the United States Agency for International Development's (USAID) disability policy, and the Convention on the Rights of Persons with Disabilities (CRPD) and discusses their application to U.S. foreign assistance programs. It examines the work of USAID, the U.S. Department of State (DOS), and the U.S. Department of Defense (DOD), and provides recommendations that will strengthen the operation of these agencies by ensuring that U.S. government funding is accessible to and inclusive of people with disabilities.

NCD's recommendations are grounded in a basic premise: that overseas economic development will not be successful unless people with disabilities are included. If development is not inclusive, the significant numbers of people with disabilities in developing countries will hinder the very economic growth the US is trying to foster. Throughout our report, NCD urges micro-level interventions aimed at income generation and macro-level interventions designed to create legal and regulatory frameworks that are accessible to people with disabilities.

In many countries, domestic law contains blatant discriminatory provisions for people with disabilities that undermine access to justice and full participation in society. The provisions that discriminate against people with disabilities include arbitrary exclusions in electoral codes, sweeping plenary guardianship laws with no due-process protections, discriminatory banking practices, and inaccessible court proceedings. National disability legal frameworks remain underdeveloped throughout the world.

In this report, NCD also finds that the failure to build infrastructure that is accessible to people with disabilities results in exclusion from physical premises as well as denial of equal access to services and resources. The barriers have a negative impact on other development work as people with disabilities may not be able to access voting centers, courthouses, administrative agencies, schools, and embassies. NCD notes that improved access to embassies will have the domestic benefit of facilitating the employment of Americans with disabilities in the Foreign Service, as ambassadors, legal advisors, political officers, and development practitioners. Accessibility to federal buildings and U.S. government-funded infrastructure projects for people with disabilities will also foster important linkages between the United States and foreign governments.

In closing, NCD commends your Administration for signing the first human rights treaty of the 21st century. The goals of this report closely correspond to one of the core mandates of the CRPD - that international development projects be inclusive of and accessible to people with disabilities. We look forward to working with you in ensuring the goals of the CRPD are met, and the recommendations in this report are implemented.

Sincerely,
Jonathan Young,
Ph.D., J.D. Chairman

LIST OF ACRONYMS

AAPD   Acquisition and Assistance Policy Directives
ABA   Architectural Barriers Act of 1968
ADA   Americans with Disabilities Act of 1990
ADAAG   Americans with Disabilities Act Accessibility Guidelines
ADS   USAID's Automated Directive System
AFRICOM   Africa Command

AJ	Administrative judge
AO	Agreement Officer
CO	Contracting Officer
CRA	Civil Rights Act of 1964
CRPD	Convention on the Rights of Persons with Disabilities
CSO	Civil society organization
DG	USAID Democracy and Governance programming
DOD	U.S. Department of Defense
DOS	U.S. Department of State
DPO	Disabled people's organization
DRI	Disability Rights International
DRL	DOS Bureau of Democracy, Human Rights, and Labor
EEOC	Equal Employment Opportunity Commission
EIT	Electronic and information technology
FOG	Field Operations Guide
GAO	Government Accountability Office
HI	Handicap International
IDEA	Individuals with Disabilities Education Act
MED	DOS Office of Medical Services
MIUSA	Mobility International USA
NCD	National Council on Disability
NGO	Nongovernmental organization
ODA	Official development assistance
OFDA	Office of U.S. Foreign Disaster Assistance
OHDACA	Overseas Humanitarian, Disaster, and Civic Aid
PMP	Project Monitoring Plan
PVO	Private voluntary organization
QDDR	Quadrennial Diplomacy and Development Review
QDR	Quadrennial Defense Review
RFA	Request for Application
RFP	Request for Proposal
TTY	teletypewriter
UN	United Nations
USAID	United States Agency for International Development

EXECUTIVE SUMMARY

The overarching aim of this report is to advance understanding and to promote accessibility and inclusion of people with disabilities in foreign assistance programs funded by the United States. The report reviews U.S. federal disability laws, the United States Agency for International Development's (USAID) Disability Policy, and the Convention on the Rights of Persons with Disabilities (CRPD) and discusses their application to U.S. foreign assistance programs. The report examines the work of USAID, the U.S. Department of State (DOS), and the U.S. Department of Defense (DOD), and provides recommendations that will strengthen the operation of these agencies by ensuring U.S. Government funding is used in a manner that is accessible to and inclusive of people with disabilities.

More than one billion people, 15 percent of the world's population, have a disability. The number continues to grow as a result of aging populations, poverty, armed conflict, and AIDS. Postconflict and developing countries have a significant proportion of people with disabilities. Although people with disabilities make up a large segment of the population in many countries, they continue to face horrific forms of discrimination and segregation throughout the world.

The United States has been a leader in advancing the rights of people with disabilities and must continue to promote disability rights through its international development work. The United States invests billions of taxpayer dollars each year into foreign assistance programs that foster international diplomacy and development. Notably, these programs develop economies, promote democracy and governance, provide humanitarian assistance, build new infrastructure, and advance and protect human rights. The United States cannot effectively accomplish the goals of foreign assistance programs unless it undertakes measures to ensure that the programs are accessible to and inclusive of people with disabilities.

To ensure effective and sustainable economic development and poverty eradication, people with disabilities must benefit from economic development programs. Micro-level interventions aimed at income generation and macro-level interventions designed to create legal and regulatory frameworks must be accessible to people with disabilities.

Further, it is important to ensure that people with disabilities are included in humanitarian assistance and disaster relief programs. Armed conflict and natural disaster increase the number of people with disabilities by causing injury, impairment, and trauma. Additionally, people with disabilities are disproportionately affected during disaster and armed conflict owing to inaccessible information dissemination and transportation procedures.

The goals of democracy and governance programs cannot be achieved without the inclusion of people with disabilities. In many countries, domestic law contains blatant discriminatory provisions for people with disabilities that undermine access to justice and full participation in society. The provisions that discriminate against people with disabilities include arbitrary exclusions in electoral codes, sweeping plenary guardianship laws with no due-process protections, discriminatory banking practices, and inaccessible court proceedings. National disability legal frameworks remain underdeveloped throughout the world.

The failure to build infrastructure that is accessible to people with disabilities results in exclusion from physical premises as well as denial of equal access to services and resources. The barriers have a negative impact on other development work as people with disabilities may not be able to access voting centers, courthouses, administrative agencies, schools, and embassies. Improved access to embassies and missions can facilitate the employment of Americans with disabilities in the Foreign Service, as ambassadors, legal advisors, political officers, and development practitioners. Accessibility to federal buildings and U.S.-Government-funded infrastructure projects for people with disabilities will foster important linkages between the United States and foreign governments.

In 2010, DOS released the inaugural Quadrennial Diplomacy and Development Review (QDDR), which articulates the future diplomatic and development goals of DOS and USAID. The QDDR underscores the importance of disability inclusion in both the programs and policies of DOS and USAID. The reform agenda set forth in the QDDR presents an opportunity and a challenge for including people with disabilities in the work of DOS and USAID.

The United States has in place the legal framework to ensure access to and inclusion of people with disabilities in foreign assistance programs. The Rehabilitation Act of 1973 prohibits federal agencies from discriminating based on disability and requires that reasonable accommodations be provided in programs under contract with the Federal Government and recipients of federal financial assistance. Significantly, Section 504 of the act protects qualified individuals with disabilities employed by programs that receive federal financial assistance. In 2003, the National Council on Disability (NCD) underscored that Section 504 applies to conduct outside of the United States. Accordingly the United States is obligated to comply with Section 504 in its foreign-assistance programs. The protections set forth for federal employees in Section 501, to federal contractors in Section 503, and to federal electronic information technology in Section 508 likewise extend to foreign assistance programs. U.S. Government agencies should comply with these sections of law and relevant regulations in operations overseas.

Beyond the Rehabilitation Act of 1973, federal disability law provides other guarantees applicable to foreign assistance programming. Title I of the Americans with Disabilities Act of 1990 (ADA) protects Americans with disabilities who work for American-owned companies overseas. Title III of the ADA requires that reasonable modifications be made for people with disabilities to enjoy full and equal access to public accommodations funded by U.S.-controlled companies. The U.S. Architectural Barriers Act of 1968 (ABA) requires that all federal buildings, including buildings financed by the Federal Government and U.S. military construction programs be accessible to people with disabilities.

In addition to the federal disability rights laws that apply to foreign assistance programs, USAID has a Disability Policy that prohibits discrimination against people with disabilities and requires inclusion in all programs and activities. Two Acquisition and Assistance Policy Directives (AAPDs) require all Requests for Applications (RFAs) and Requests for Proposals (RFPs) that involve new construction to include a provision on the Disability Policy and provide accessibility guidelines.

Finally, the United States has signed the Convention on the Rights of Persons with Disabilities. The research goals of this report closely correspond to one of the core mandates of the CRPD, that international development projects be inclusive of and accessible to people with disabilities. Article 32 of the CRPD requires States Parties to integrate people with disabilities into all aspects of their assistance programs, from the design stage through implementation. The CRPD provides the United States with a tool to promote nondiscrimination and equality for people with disabilities worldwide through its foreign assistance programs.

Summary of Methodology

This report provides a comprehensive overview of the current state of knowledge, attitudes, and practices toward people with disabilities in U.S.-funded overseas facilities, programs, and employment opportunities. The study was designed to elicit information from a range of stakeholders working in the field of international development. The research methodology for this report included key informant interviews, focus groups, in-country assessments, and extensive desk-based document review. The research also included a legal analysis of the extraterritorial application of U.S. federal disability laws and the implications of the CRPD for U.S. foreign assistance programs. The three primary U.S. Government agencies that were reviewed for this report were USAID, DOS, and DOD.

In the early stages of research, 20 countries were selected for in-country assessments of U.S. Government-funded facilities, programs, and employment practices. Local advocates of disability rights visited U.S. embassies and USAID missions in 14 of the 20 countries, where they conducted interviews and accessibility assessments. Accessibility assessments covered, among other things, the accessibility of entrances, hallways, and bathrooms; the availability of sign language interpreters; and whether information and materials were provided or available in accessible formats. While a limited number of countries were selected for the in-country reviews, the more general, sector-specific analyses included desk-based document review of many additional countries. The research was conducted with the intention of generating as broad an overview of current policy and practice as possible.

The study examined four major sectors of international development funded by the U.S. Government: (1) humanitarian assistance and disaster relief; (2) democracy and governance; (3) economic growth; and (4) cultural exchange programs. In-country interviews of USAID personnel were specifically geared toward democracy and governance programming. The other sectors were reviewed through extensive desk-based research, as well as interviews with federal employees and government contractors with headquarters in Washington, DC. Additionally, a roundtable event for key stakeholders who work in the field of disability rights and international development enabled participants to share their opinions on inclusive development.

Summary of Findings

- USAID has initiated various efforts to promote disability-inclusive development. Although USAID has advanced disability inclusion, many USAID employees have low levels of awareness about disability issues and limited understanding of how to include people with disabilities in programs. Many USAID personnel are unaware of the Disability Policy. Personnel who are aware of the policy are unable to clearly articulate its relevance or impact on their work.

• The majority of USAID-funded projects that include people with disabilities are stand-alone, disability-specific projects with small budgets. USAID uses a "twin-track" approach to disability inclusion by funding small disability-specific projects and promoting disability inclusion in general development programs. Through this approach, very few general development programs successfully implement disability components. The main goal of inclusive development is to ensure that all U.S. Government-funded programs are accessible to and inclusive of people with disabilities. USAID's current twin-track approach does not effectively foster inclusion in all programs and in some ways promotes segregated disability-specific projects with no relationship to general development programs operated out of the same USAID mission. NCD found that disability-specific projects have been effective on a small scale in building the capacity of disabled people's organizations (DPOs) and promoting the rights of people with disabilities, but disability-specific projects have not successfully been integrated with general development programs. NCD emphasizes the importance of ensuring that all foreign assistance programs include people with disabilities.

• Although USAID's disability-specific projects have successfully developed monitoring and evaluation strategies, the majority of USAID general development programs do not apply a disability lens in a consistent and ongoing manner to monitoring and evaluation efforts.

• Many USAID technical publications fail to provide guidance on how to include people with disabilities in projects, thereby undermining the implementation of USAID's Disability Policy.

• The Department of State Country Reports on Human Rights show marked improvement in their coverage of country human rights conditions affecting the rights of people with disabilities; however, many reports do not provide consistent, credible information or are seriously limited in their scope.

• Security and other concerns trump accessibility measures, with the effect that officials at embassies, consular offices, and missions routinely invoke security in response to the failure of facilities and services to be fully accessible to people with disabilities. For example, in many embassies the push-button doors were turned off because of security concerns. A push-button door is commonly found on the side of doorways for people who use wheelchairs to push in order to automatically open the door. Many secure buildings in the United States have this feature, and they are fully operational. It is unacceptable to allow security concerns to trump accessibility for people with disabilities in overseas buildings.

• Information and materials are not provided in accessible formats at embassies, consular offices, and missions in order to facilitate full access to facilities and services for people with disabilities.

• Cultural exchange programs do not routinely provide information on programs in accessible formats, including information concerning accessible housing options.

Summary of Recommendations

The following recommendations are based on this report's findings and focus on the accessibility of U.S. foreign assistance programs for people with disabilities in areas covered in the research. This section summarizes the recommendations, with more detail provided in part 9 of this report. NCD directs its recommendations to the Administration, Congress, USAID, DOS, and DOD. The recommendations also have relevance for other U.S. Government agencies operating abroad, and those agencies should also implement many of these recommendations. These recommendations will advance accessibility and inclusion for people with disabilities and will improve the effectiveness and impact of U.S.-funded foreign assistance throughout the world.

NCD calls on the Administration to recognize the extraterritorial application of Sections 501, 503, 504, and 508 of the Rehabilitation Act; Title III of the Americans with Disabilities Act; and the Architectural Barriers Act. Measures should be undertaken to ensure that all U.S. Government-funded foreign assistance work is brought into compliance with these laws.

NCD Recommendations Directed to Congress

1) Congress should instruct USAID, DOS, DOD, and other U.S. Government agencies operating overseas that Sections 501, 503, 504, and 508 of the Rehabilitation Act of 1973 apply to overseas programs and employment opportunities operated by the U.S. Government.

2) Congress should instruct USAID, DOS, DOD, and other U.S. Government agencies operating overseas to promote greater comparative knowledge and understanding of local disability law and policy frameworks, including the status of CRPD ratification in countries receiving foreign assistance.

3) Congress should narrow the waivers and exceptions currently outlined in the Architectural Barriers Act of 1968 and regulations for building temporary structures in times of emergency.

4) The U.S. Senate, upon receipt of the ratification package, should consider and expeditiously provide its advice and consent to ratification of the Convention on the Rights of Persons with Disabilities.

NCD Recommendations Directed to USAID, DOS, and DOD

5) USAID, DOS, and DOD should implement mandatory disability rights and disability inclusion in development training sessions for employees at all missions and embassies. The findings of this report indicate that personnel around the world are unfamiliar with strategies for disability inclusion in facilities, programs, and employment opportunities. Ensuring the participation of people with disabilities, DPOs, and inclusive-development experts should be a core component of any training strategy.

6) USAID, DOS, and DOD should promote employment opportunities for people with disabilities in missions, embassies, consular offices, and overseas programs. Americans with disabilities have the right to equal access to employment opportunities and are entitled to reasonable accommodations to perform their job duties. This should include the opportunity to work in U.S. embassies, missions, and U.S.-Government funded programs abroad. Further, where local nationals are utilized, local nationals with disabilities should be hired to work in U.S.-funded overseas programs and facilities to promote greater inclusion of people with disabilities in U.S.-funded foreign assistance programs.

NCD Recommendations Directed to USAID

7) USAID should review and update its Disability Policy. The current policy, drafted in 1997, is outdated and provides minimal guidance on how USAID programs can be made inclusive across all sectors of its development portfolio.

8) USAID should provide adequate resources for the Coordinator on Disability and Inclusive Development to accomplish the goals of the USAID Disability Policy.

9) USAID should ensure that all of its programs are accessible to and inclusive of people with disabilities. To this end, USAID should undertake measures to advance inclusion beyond disability-specific projects. Disability-specific projects should be integrated into large-scale general development programs. Further, organizations with expertise to develop disability-specific projects should participate in the design and implementation of large general development programs.

10) USAID should issue a policy directive that requires meaningful disability inclusion in the statements of work and program descriptions of RFPs and RFAs.

11) USAID should include people with disabilities in the technical approach section of evaluation criteria for RFAs and RFPs. Such an approach will compel applicants and offerors to emphasize their technical approach to disability inclusion and implementation of the Disability Policy.

12) USAID should apply a disability lens to its monitoring and evaluation efforts. To this end, USAID should require applicants and offerors to develop and outline disability indicators and outputs in result frameworks and performance management plans. Given the commitment to strengthening USAID's monitoring and evaluation, as underscored in USAID Forward and the QDDR, such an approach is timely and readily achievable.

13) USAID should provide specific instructions for applicants and offerors in the preparation of the budget proposal in all USAID solicitations for costing reasonable accommodations and modifications for people with disabilities. A line item in the cost proposal for proper budgeting of reasonable accommodations should be specified in these instructions and in accompanying charts or spreadsheets.

14) USAID should fund capacity building for DPOs as a part of its civil society-strengthening program within the Democracy and Governance sector. Consistent with USAID's work to mobilize constituencies for reform through civil society organization (CSO) development, USAID should redouble its efforts to provide funding to DPOs to build their capacity to undertake disability law and policy reform,

collaborate with partner organizations, manage funds, research funding opportunities, and draft proposals, among other skills that are essential to sustain inclusive development programs.

NCD Recommendations Directed to DOS

15) DOS should issue an official policy statement on compliance requirements for Sections 501, 503, 504, and 508 of the Rehabilitation Act. DOS must make it clear to all federal employees that Sections 501, 503, 504, and 508 apply to all U.S. programs, facilities, and employment opportunities overseas.

16) DOS should provide adequate resources for the Office of the Special Advisor on International Disability Rights to effectively promote disability inclusion in all aspects of DOS work.

17) DOS should ensure that all embassies, consular offices, and missions are fully accessible to people with disabilities. Entranceways, meeting rooms, bathrooms, and other areas must be accessible to people with disabilities. Information and materials must also be accessible and available to people with disabilities. This includes visa applications, websites, and informational pamphlets and brochures, among other materials distributed to the public by embassies, consular offices, and missions. Additionally, DOS should ensure that where accessible architectural modifications already exist in buildings, they are made fully operational and are not disregarded owing to security or other concerns.

18) DOS should strengthen its disability rights coverage in its Human Rights Reports. Human Rights Officers should be encouraged to consult with local DPOs when drafting Country Reports within its Human Rights Reports.

19) DOS should support trainings for staff of cultural exchange programs on the inclusion of people with disabilities and consider adopting specific disability-inclusive mission statements or policies that encourage qualified people with disabilities to apply. DOS should ensure that all information on programs is available in accessible alternative formats (website materials, print, and in person) and that accessible housing options are available for participants with disabilities, along with individualized accommodations.

NCD Recommendations Directed to DOD

20) DOD should limit the number of waivers and exceptions permitted under its newly adopted ABA Accessibility Standards for DOD Facilities. Waivers and exceptions have been used throughout the world to build inaccessible infrastructure that later must be retrofitted to provide accessibility at a high cost to American taxpayers.

21) DOD should provide clear guidance to contractors on the application of the ABA Accessibility Standards in developing countries. At present, the standards state that they apply "worldwide," but there is a gap in the standards that allows contractors to apply for waivers or argue for an exception in developing countries. These standards must clearly indicate that DOD infrastructure projects in foreign countries are subject to the same provisions as other DOD infrastructure projects.

PART 1. INTRODUCTION AND BACKGROUND

"[W]e cannot fulfill both the moral and the economic imperatives of development unless we universalize the opportunities we help to create. [We] will work to mainstream disability perspectives throughout the programs and policies of State and USAID, respectively."—Quadrennial Diplomacy and Development Review, *Leading Through Civilian Power*, U.S. Department of State and USAID (December 2010).

The Situation of People with Disabilities in Developing Countries

The *World Report on Disability*, released in 2011 by the World Health Organization and the World Bank, reveals that more than one billion people, 15 percent of the world's population, have a disability.[1] The report discloses that the global population of people with disabilities is higher than previously estimated, and that the population is continuing to grow.[2]

The experience of disability for people living in developing countries is more profound than for those in developed countries. As the *World Report on Disability* notes, disability disproportionately affects vulnerable populations:

Results from the World Health Survey indicate a higher disability prevalence in lower income countries than in higher income countries.

People from the poorest wealth quintile, women, and older people also have a higher prevalence of disability. People who have a low income, are out of work, or have low educational qualifications are at an increased risk of disability.[3]

Furthermore, studies estimate that only 2 percent of people with disabilities in developing countries have access to rehabilitation and appropriate basic services.[4] Research suggests that only 2 to 3 percent of children with disabilities attend schools in developing countries.[5] Poverty and social exclusion lead to multiple disadvantages and forms of discrimination in other spheres, including employment, housing, and participation in community life.[6] The barriers that limit the participation of people with disabilities also preclude their participation in development-planning decisions that could advance their inclusion in society.[7]

The situation of people with disabilities in developing countries underscores the critical need to ensure that foreign assistance programming is directed toward advancing disability rights and eliminating barriers to inclusion for people with disabilities. The importance of ensuring the participation of people with disabilities in foreign assistance programming has been further exposed by the increased attention to the human rights of people with disabilities and the prevalence of disability discrimination worldwide,[8] prompted in part by the adoption of the Convention on the Rights of Persons with Disabilities[9] by the United Nations in 2006. The failure to reach this significant population in foreign assistance programming impacts a large segment of society in developing countries and is beginning to emerge as a major concern among numerous bilateral and multilateral development agencies around the world.[10]

The Role of the United States

The United States has an important role to play in improving the situation of people with disabilities throughout the world. The United States contributes substantial funding to foreign assistance and has in place the legal framework to ensure that people with disabilities can both access and benefit from such assistance. American disability rights laws provide essential guidance for U.S. Government agencies in implementing foreign assistance programs that are inclusive and accessible to people with disabilities. Further, it is the stated policy of USAID to make development, stability, and humanitarian assistance efforts accessible to all.[11] The United States is a signatory to the Convention on the Rights of Persons with Disabilities (CRPD), and significantly, the CRPD requires that international development programs be inclusive of people with disabilities.[12] As the world's largest bilateral development donor[13] and a world leader in domestic disability rights law and policy, the United States should ensure that taxpayer dollars support foreign assistance programs that are inclusive of and accessible to people with disabilities.

In 2010 the U.S. Department of State (DOS) released the Quadrennial Diplomacy and Development Review (QDDR),[14] modeled on the Quadrennial Defense Review (QDR).[15] The QDDR focuses on four components of reform for both DOS and USAID:

1) Adapt international diplomacy to new threats and opportunities;
2) Transform development assistance to deliver results and reestablish USAID as the world's premier development agency;
3) Improve the ability of the United States to operate in fragile states and help stop conflicts before they happen; and
4) Improve approaches to planning, procurement, and personnel.

Significantly, the inaugural QDDR articulates the future diplomatic and development goals of DOS and USAID, underscores the importance of including people with disabilities, and commits to disability inclusion in both the programs and policies of DOS and USAID.[16] The reform agenda set forth in the QDDR clearly presents both an opportunity as well as a challenge for disability inclusion in the work of DOS and USAID.

Purpose and Structure of Report

The purpose of this report is to assess the implementation of disability inclusion in U.S. Government-funded overseas facilities, programs, and employment opportunities. In particular, the report analyzes how U.S. federal disability law and policy applies to U.S. foreign assistance work and reviews the application of disability inclusion in three specific areas of U.S. foreign assistance: (1) accessibility of U.S.-funded overseas construction and infrastructure projects; (2) access to and inclusion of people with disabilities in U.S.-funded international development programs; and (3) employment opportunities for people with disabilities. The report also reviews the relevance of international development provisions under the CRPD, of which the United States is a signatory and may ratify in the future. Given the ratification of the CRPD in more than 100 countries around the world, including many countries where the U.S. Government is a major donor of foreign assistance, the CRPD provisions on disability inclusive development assume particular significance.

The report focuses on the work of USAID, DOS, and the U.S. Department of Defense (DOD), as they contribute the bulk of U.S. funding overseas. However, many of the recommendations here are equally relevant for other U.S. Government agencies that fund programs overseas.

Following the introduction, the report is divided into nine parts. part 2 lays out the research methodology used in the study. part 3 considers U.S. federal disability rights laws and their application to federal foreign assistance programming. part 4 provides an analysis of disability-inclusive development within the context of international disability rights standards, including the CRPD. part 5 reviews the USAID Disability Policy and how it is currently being implemented in development programs. part 6 provides an overview of selected sectors of USAID's development programming, as well as an analysis of how accessible and inclusive those sectors are to people with disabilities. part 7 focuses on DOS and reviews its Country Human Rights Reports as well as embassy accessibility and cultural exchange programs. part 8 reviews laws and policies used by DOD in overseas building and infrastructure efforts. The report concludes by setting forth recommendations that will secure continued U.S. leadership in inclusive development.

PART 2. RESEARCH METHODOLOGY

In the development of a comprehensive overview of the current state of knowledge, attitudes, and practices toward people with disabilities in U.S.-funded overseas facilities, programs, and employment opportunities, the study was designed to elicit information from a range of stakeholders who work in the field of international development. The research methodology included key informant interviews, focus groups, in-country assessments, and extensive desk-based document review. The research design also included a legal analysis of the extraterritorial application of U.S. federal disability laws and the implications of the CRPD for U.S. foreign assistance programs. While the research was focused on compiling information on whether and how U.S. Government agencies ensure accessibility and inclusion for people with disabilities in foreign assistance, it does not attempt to provide a comprehensive review of the multitude of U.S. Government-funded foreign assistance efforts. The three primary U.S. Government agencies that were reviewed for the purposes of this report were USAID, DOS, and DOD. The scope of research had slight variations for each agency in an effort to review the broad array of U.S.-Government funded foreign assistance work and develop concrete recommendations that are applicable to all U.S. Government agencies working overseas.

In the early stages of research, 20 countries[17] were selected for in-country assessments of U.S.-Government funded facilities, programs, and employment practices. The following criteria were used in the selection in order to achieve a diverse group of countries representative of where the United States currently invests in foreign assistance programming: (1) geographic diversity; (2) diversity in development programming; (3) the amount of U.S. Government foreign assistance funding; and (4) strength of local DPOs. While a limited number of countries were selected for the in-country reviews, the more general, sector-specific analyses included desk-based document review. Other research into many additional countries was conducted with the intention of generating as broad an overview as possible of current policy and practice.

Local disability rights advocates (local advocates) conducted in-country assessments in 14 of the 20 countries studied. The local advocates visited U.S. embassies and USAID missions, where they conducted interviews and accessibility assessments.[18] The interview questions were semistructured and geared toward learning whether and how people with disabilities are included in development programs, as well as gaining a sense of USAID and DOS employee knowledge about disability issues. There were separate questions for embassy and mission personnel. Furthermore, local advocates conducted brief assessments of embassy premises to determine how accessible they were to people with various types of disabilities. Accessibility assessments included coverage of, among other things, the accessibility of entrances, hallways, and bathrooms; the availability of sign language interpreters; and whether information and materials were provided or available in accessible formats.[19]

In addition to in-country research, a series of interviews, meetings, and focus groups were conducted in Washington, DC, to elicit additional information about disability inclusion and accessibility in the foreign development projects and policies implemented by the three agencies reviewed in this study.

This study examined four major sectors of international development funded by the U.S. Government: (1) humanitarian assistance and disaster relief; (2) democracy and governance; (3) economic growth; and (4) cultural exchange programs. In-country interviews of USAID personnel were specifically geared toward democracy and governance programming. The other sectors were reviewed through extensive desk-based research,[20] interviews with agency personnel in Washington, DC, and government contractors, and a roundtable event with inclusive development program implementers.

PART 3. FEDERAL DISABILITY RIGHTS LAWS AND THEIR APPLICATION TO OVERSEAS FACILITIES, PROGRAMS, AND EMPLOYMENT

This part examines federal disability rights laws and evaluates the extent to which they apply to U.S. Government-funded overseas facilities, programs, and employment. It also considers whether and how such laws apply to private entities abroad. In particular, the protections afforded by the Americans with Disabilities Act (ADA)[21] and the Rehabilitation Act of 1973[22] are discussed in relation to international development work funded by the United States.

Federal Disability Rights Laws: An Overview

The United States has a long history of leadership in the development of progressive disability law and policy and in working to ensure the equal rights of Americans with disabilities. In 1973, Congress enacted the Rehabilitation Act, the first federal legislation to protect the civil rights of people with disabilities and the first domestic legislation in the world to introduce the concept of reasonable accommodation.[23] The Rehabilitation Act prohibits discrimination based on disability by federal agencies and requires that reasonable accommodations be provided in programs under contract with the Federal Government and recipients of federal financial assistance.[24]

In 1990, Congress enacted the Americans with Disabilities Act, which further extended the protections and prohibitions of the Rehabilitation Act to private conduct with the goal of reducing the social discrimination and stigma faced by people with disabilities.[25] In drafting the ADA, Congress recognized that "historically, society tended to isolate and segregate individuals with disabilities, and, despite some improvements, such forms of discrimination against individuals with disabilities continue to be a serious and pervasive social problem."[26] The ADA prohibits discrimination in the following areas: (1) employment; (2) public services; (3) telecommunications; (4) higher education; (5) professional examinations and licensing; (6) access to public accommodations and commercial facilities; and (7) other realms of society.[27] The ADA is divided into several titles that cover the various protections afforded by the law.[28] Titles I and III cover employment and access to public accommodations and are thus most relevant for the purposes of this study, in particular their application to U.S. Government-funded facilities, programs, and employment overseas.

Title I of the ADA specifically prohibits discrimination on the basis of disability in private employment. Title I requires employers to provide "reasonable accommodations" for people with disabilities in the employment realm. Reasonable accommodations by private employers include, but are not limited to—

- Providing job application materials in accessible formats;
- Providing assistive technology for people with disabilities so they can perform the essential functions of their job;
- Providing interpreters for communication for people with disabilities and their colleagues; and
- Providing accessible workspace for people with disabilities.

Title III of the ADA requires "reasonable modifications" be made to ensure that people with disabilities can fully and equally enjoy "public accommodations."[29] Under Title III, any entity that leases, owns, or operates a public accommodation must make reasonable modifications to its premises that are necessary for people with disabilities to access goods, services, facilities, privileges, advantages, or accommodations. Examples of Title III violations include a private university that does not accept students with disabilities, a bank that does not have an accessible entranceway, and a privately owned medical facility that does not provide people who are deaf with sign language interpreters upon request.

The ADA and Rehabilitation Act, in combination with other key pieces of federal disability legislation, including the Individuals with Disabilities Education Act (IDEA),[30] the Fair Housing Amendments Act,[31] the Architectural Barriers Act of 1968,[32] the Air Carrier Access Act,[33] and the Telecommunications Act of 1996,[34] comprise the core of federal disability rights legislation. One of the issues examined in detail in this report is the extent to which American federal disability rights laws apply extraterritorially—beyond the borders of the United States—and the implications of extraterritoriality on U.S. Government-funded foreign assistance programs. This review is particularly important because the U.S. Government is the largest international development donor and should ensure compliance with U.S. disability rights laws in overseas work. Moreover, Americans with disabilities work and travel abroad, whether as private citizens, as diplomats, or as implementers of U.S.-funded foreign assistance programs, and must be able to enjoy equal access to overseas facilities, programs, and employment.

Extraterritorial Application of Federal Disability Rights Law

In reviewing the extraterritorial application of American disability rights laws to determine whether and how they apply to U.S. Government-funded overseas facilities, programs, and employment, a central question is whether Americans with disabilities are afforded the same protections abroad as those they are accorded in the United States. A key consideration, therefore, is whether U.S. Government-funded facilities, programs, and employment opportunities overseas must comport with the Rehabilitation Act of 1973 and other federal laws to the same extent as U.S. Government-funded facilities, programs, and employment opportunities *within* the United States. The Supreme Court has held that Congress has the authority to enact laws that apply outside the territorial boundaries of the United States.[35] Historically, however, many American courts have been reluctant to apply federal laws extraterritorially, relying on the long-held presumption against extraterritorial application of federal laws. Under this presumption, and absent explicit affirmative congressional intent of extraterritorial reach, U.S. courts traditionally have not applied federal laws to actions or parties outside of the United States.[36]

As the United States became more involved in the global economy, its courts slowly abandoned the presumption against extraterritorial application in matters that ranged from antitrust enforcement against foreign businesses to international trademark infringement, and in some cases, criminal law.[37] Further, U.S. courts started reviewing legislative history[38] to determine whether Congress intended for a law to apply outside of U.S. borders.[39] For the purposes of this report, it is important to consider how courts have interpreted congressional intent with regard to federal civil rights statutes in claims arising in foreign jurisdictions, as many American civil rights laws, including the majority of federal disability rights laws, are silent when it comes to defining their extraterritorial reach.

In 1991, the Supreme Court considered the issue of extraterritorial application of American civil rights law in *EEOC v. Arabian Am. Oil Co. (Aramco)*.[40] *Aramco* involved application of Title VII of the 1964 Civil Rights Act (CRA) to a foreign-born American worker employed by an American corporation overseas.[41] The employee alleged employment discrimination based on his religion and national origin.[42] The Court relied on the presumption against extraterritoriality to hold that federal statutes did not apply abroad "unless a contrary intent appears."[43] Significantly, the Court noted that Congress had the authority to extend the protections of American civil rights laws to American citizens working for American employers abroad.[44] However, the *Aramco* Court held that Congress had not issued a "clear statement" as to the extraterritorial reach when Title VII was enacted.[45] Because there was no clear language that Congress intended Title VII to apply to conduct outside the United States, the Supreme Court was not willing to extend the law's protections in that case.[46]

In direct response to *Aramco*, Congress moved to enact amendments to the Civil Rights Act of 1991 (CRA Amendments) that specifically overturned the Court's decision.[47] The CRA Amendments expanded the protections of Title I of the ADA and Title VII of the CRA to Americans working for American corporations and companies controlled by American corporations overseas.[48] The CRA Amendments extended protections to people with disabilities in the private employment realm under Title I of the ADA and did not specifically apply to other U.S. disability laws, such as the Rehabilitation Act of 1973 or other titles of the ADA.[49] Nevertheless, the 1991 Civil Rights Amendments exemplified Congress' discontent with the Supreme Court's interpretation of the reach of civil rights laws and laid the foundation for finding that the protections articulated in federal disability rights laws should apply overseas.

Notwithstanding these developments, important questions remained as to the scope of protections and rights afforded under federal disability rights laws when applied overseas. As noted in NCD's 2003 report, *Foreign Policy and Disability: Legislative Strategies and Civil Rights Protections to Ensure Inclusion of People with Disabilities (Foreign Policy and Disability)*:

> Recent case law indicates that courts may be willing to extend the protections of American disability discrimination laws to persons and conduct overseas, even in the absence of specific legislative language,

and even in the face of the long-held presumption against the extraterritorial application of American laws.[50]

Since 2003, U.S. courts have continued to apply American disability laws extraterritorially. In 2005, the Supreme Court addressed the issue of extraterritorial application of the ADA to foreign-flagged cruise ships in *Spector v. Norwegian Cruise Line Ltd. (Spector)*.[51] In *Spector*, the plaintiffs brought claims against a cruise line company alleging violations of Title III of the ADA.[52] The Court considered the issue of whether Title III applies to foreign-flagged cruise ships.[53] The Court held that because of the business practices of Norwegian Cruise Lines in the United States, and the fact that the majority of their patrons were American citizens, the foreign company could be held liable under Title III. In so holding, the Court struck down a lower court's ruling that the ADA was "inapplicable because the statute has no clear statement or explicit text mandating coverage for foreign-flag ships in U.S. waters."[54]

In *Spector*, the Court noted that if extraterritorial application was provided in a federal statute, then the court must enforce the statute. However, the Court abandoned the "clear statement" rule that looked only to whether a federal disability statute expressly mentioned applying extraterritorially. *Spector* is thus highly relevant, given that many American disability statutes are silent as to their application overseas. The *Spector* decision gives courts more discretion to analyze disability rights claims arising abroad on a case-by-case basis to determine if Congress intended to prevent the alleged disability discrimination extraterritorially.

Although U.S. federal disability statutes are silent as to whether they can be applied extraterritorially, congressional intent in creating the ADA and other federal disability statutes was to promote the full participation of people with disabilities in all facets of society and to protect people with disabilities from discrimination that would limit such participation.[55] In 2008, Congress amended the ADA to reemphasize the law's purpose to focus on preventing discrimination and to correct the Supreme Court's previous errors in statutory interpretation that narrowed the ADA's application.[56] Congressional intent discloses that American disability rights laws should be interpreted to provide the same protections and remedies to Americans with disabilities throughout the world. The extraterritorial application of American disability rights laws is essential to ensuring that Americans with disabilities can travel, live, and work anywhere they want to in the world. One example that illustrates the importance of these laws applying abroad occurs when an American with a disability encounters an emergency in a foreign country and needs to be able to access the U.S. embassy in the country.

Accessibility of Federal Buildings and New Construction Projects Overseas

New investments in infrastructure funded by U.S. taxpayers should not create barriers that will hinder the participation of Americans in work and tourism abroad. Nor should such investments create barriers in countries whose development the United States is seeking to promote. In other words, the failure to provide access results in exclusion from physical premises as well as denial of equal access to services and resources inside buildings. Lack of access to public buildings also infringes on political rights by preventing access to voting centers, courthouses, administrative agencies, and embassies. Further, access to embassies and missions can facilitate the employment of Americans with disabilities in the Foreign Service, as ambassadors, legal advisors, political officers, and development practitioners, among other positions. Thus, ensuring accessibility to federal buildings for people with disabilities can help foster important linkages between the United States and foreign governments.

The Architectural Barriers Act of 1968 requires that all federal buildings be made accessible.[57] The law requires that all buildings designed, constructed, or financed by the Federal Government ensure physical accessibility.[58] The law contains no provision limiting its applicability to buildings located in the United States, and accordingly, should be construed as applying to embassies and missions overseas.[59] Further, the concept of universal design should be applied to all U.S.-funded new construction overseas. The next part provides an in-depth review of the concept of universal design as defined in the CRPD.

Equal Access to Employment Opportunities in U.S.-Funded Overseas Programs

Under American disability rights laws, Americans with disabilities have the right to equal access to employment opportunities and are entitled to reasonable accommodations to perform their job duties. This should include the opportunity to work in U.S. embassies, missions, and U.S. Government-funded programs abroad. It is therefore important for U.S. Government agencies to ensure that Americans with disabilities are afforded the same protections and remedies overseas as in the United States. The following analysis reviews the provisions of the ADA and Rehabilitation Act of 1973 that are most relevant to employment opportunities for Americans with disabilities in overseas programs.

Title I of the ADA applies to private employers and provides, "[n]o covered entity shall discriminate against a qualified individual on the basis of disability in regard to job application procedures, the hiring, advancement, or discharge of employees, employee compensation, job training, and other terms, conditions, and privileges of employment."[60] As discussed above, Title I of the ADA extends to protect American citizens working for private American-controlled employers overseas, such as major American corporations with offices in other countries.[61] These groups of Americans with disabilities who work abroad are afforded the same accommodations, rights, and remedies as people with disabilities working in the United States. Although Title I does not apply to the Federal Government, when private employers contract with the Federal Government to perform work overseas, private employers must comply with Title I.[62] This requirement is of special relevance for the purposes of this report given that a high percentage of U.S. Government-funded foreign assistance work is implemented by private contractors, which are considered covered entities under Title I.[63] For example, Chemonics International, a large private international development company working under USAID contracts, is subject to Title I of the ADA in the 75 countries where it works. Accordingly, Title I jurisdiction extends to protect Americans with disabilities who work for these private employers on foreign assistance programs.[64] It follows that government employees with disabilities working on the same program overseas should be covered by Section 501 of the Rehabilitation Act, the legal equivalent of Title I for government employees. Title I's protections are essential to furthering the goals of inclusive development by ensuring that more people with disabilities will work in the field of international development for both private contractors and U.S. Government agencies, thus raising disability awareness worldwide.

The Rehabilitation Act of 1973 prohibits discrimination on the basis of disability in (1) programs receiving federal financial assistance; (2) federal employment; and (3) the employment practices of federal contractors.[65]

Section 504 of the Rehabilitation Act applies to entities and programs receiving federal funding and covers "otherwise qualified individual[s] with a disability in the U.S."[66] NCD's *Foreign Policy and Disability* briefly discussed the meaning of "in the United States," and then presented arguments that recent case law demonstrates that Section 504 is applicable overseas, noting, "Upon review of recent court decisions, it appears that Section 504 also applies to conduct outside of the United States."[67] Following this line of reasoning, the U.S. Federal Government is obligated to comply with the nondiscrimination mandate of Section 504 in programs overseas, provided such compliance would not conflict with another country's laws.[68] The requirement that compliance with Section 504 not conflict with another country's laws is relevant here as it means that U.S. Government agencies must ensure their programs and practices in each country do not conflict with the host country's domestic law.[69] As will be discussed at length in the next part, the ratification of the CRPD by dozens of countries where the United States funds development programs has implications for U.S. Government agencies in their foreign assistance work. Moreover, it should be noted that the CRPD prohibits discrimination on the basis of disability and creates a duty to provide reasonable accommodations, provisions that are consistent with Section 504 of the Rehabilitation Act of 1973. The failure to comply with Section 504 in federally funded programs abroad has the perverse effect of creating an inconsistent application of a law that Congress clearly intended to apply to the U.S. Federal Government in federally funded programs, facilities, and employment opportunities. Further, the failure to apply Section 504 in foreign assistance work undermines disability laws in countries that have ratified the CRPD and seriously undercuts American leadership in disability rights and inclusive development.[70]

Similarly, Section 501 of the Rehabilitation Act, which prohibits discrimination against federal employees, has been held to apply in cases of federal employees seeking to work abroad.[71] In its 2009 decision, *Katz v. USAID and Department of State*, the Equal Employment Opportunity Commission (EEOC)[72] held that DOS and USAID were in violation of Section 501 for failing to conduct an individualized assessment of an applicant for a U.S. Foreign Service position.[73] The complainant in *Katz* alleged that DOS and USAID discriminated against her on the basis of disability when she was denied a Class 1 Medical Clearance after applying for a U.S. Foreign Service position in USAID's Democracy and Governance Office.[74] The Department of State's Office of Medical Services (MED) denied the complainant the Class 1 Clearance because she did not meet its definition of "worldwide availability," which was considered an essential function of the position.[75] According to USAID, "worldwide availability is both an affirmed willingness to serve anywhere in the world and a matter of being medically qualified to do so; both are essential requirements for appointment to the Foreign Service."[76] In cases where an individual does not receive a Class 1 Clearance, USAID's Medical Review Committee can grant a waiver if the applicant can work in more than 51 percent of worldwide posts. In *Katz,* the waiver was not granted, and therefore USAID did not hire the complainant, notwithstanding medical evidence provided by her longtime physician stating that she could indeed live and work at the post in question and irrespective of the fact that she had already worked in a difficult postconflict environment in a previous position that was, incidentally, funded by the U.S. Government.[77]

In *Katz,* the EEOC shifted the burden of proof to the agencies and provided guidance on how the agencies must conduct assessments: "when making its individualized assessment the agency must gather information and base its decision on substantial information regarding the individual's work and medical history."[78] Despite a number of letters from the complainant's physicians providing evidence that she did indeed meet the "worldwide availability" standard, two physicians at the Department of State Office of Medical Services (MED) who reviewed the complainant's medical record admitted that they never saw those letters.[79] Furthermore, the EEOC found that the MED grounded its decisions on assumptions about the complainant concerning her medical condition and did not undertake an investigation to assess whether the assumptions were true.[80] The EEOC upheld the administrative judge's (AJ's) decision and stated: "The AJ found the State Department failed to conduct an individualized assessment and hence, did not satisfy its burden of establishing complainant was a direct threat."[81] The *Katz* decision provides a salient example of how Section 501 has been applied to prohibit discrimination against federal employees with disabilities working abroad.

The *Katz* decision illustrates ongoing challenges in ensuring that employment opportunities are open to people with disabilities. In this regard, it stands to reason that Congress should instruct DOS and USAID that Section 501 applies abroad and that agencies must issue clear guidance to missions and embassies. In comparing Section 501 to Title 1 of the ADA, it is important to note that Congress made it clear in the CRA Amendments that Title I applies overseas, and thus Title I does indeed apply to private contractors who receive U.S. Government funding to implement programs. It is equally clear that Congress also intends for government employees to have the same protections, rights, and remedies as private employees working on government-funded programs and thus Congress should provide clear instructions to DOS and USAID that they must adhere to the provisions set out in Section 501.

Similarly, Section 503 of the Rehabilitation Act should also be applied to prohibit discrimination beyond the borders of the United States. Section 503 prohibits discrimination by contractors with the Federal Government,[82] and NCD's *Foreign Policy and Disability* report emphasized that it may be applied extraterritorially, even in the absence of specific legislative provision.[83] As previously discussed in relation to Title 1 of the ADA, Section 503's application to government contractors is critically important as the majority of U.S.-funded foreign assistance work is contracted out by the Federal Government to private contractors who must comply with the law's provisions. Therefore, Section 503 has a significant role to play in promoting the rights of people with disabilities to work for government contractors, and thus furthers the goal of inclusive development by creating jobs and programming accessible to people with disabilities working in international development.

Section 508 of the Rehabilitation Act of 1973 is another important provision that should be applied overseas to ensure equal access to employment for people with disabilities.[84] Section 508 covers access to electronic and information technology (EIT) procured by the Federal Government.[85] It requires that EIT developed, procured, maintained or used by any federal agency be accessible to people with disabilities. Section 508 "enhances the ability of federal employees with disabilities to have access to and use of information and data that is *comparable* to that provided to others. Similarly, agency procurement of accessible EIT enhances the ability of members of the public with disabilities who are seeking information or services from a federal agency to have access to and use of information and data that is *comparable* to that provided to others." Of specific relevance to this report, Section 508 applies to U.S. Government websites and procurements issued on the Internet.[86] U.S. embassies, missions, and other federal offices overseas should be in compliance with Section 508 and ensure that their websites are accessible to people with disabilities. Further, U.S. Government agencies operating overseas must issue electronic procurements in a manner that is accessible to people with disabilities. Websites and procurements must be in accessible formats in order to ensure equal access to programs and employment in U.S. Government-funded overseas work.

Conclusion

The proper application of American disability rights laws abroad is crucial to achieving and promoting the purposes and goals behind the ADA and Rehabilitation Act, namely, the full participation of people with disabilities in society and protection against discrimination that would limit such participation. U.S. involvement in international work and foreign aid is increasing, and the American workforce abroad should be afforded the same protections as Americans working within the United States. Further, the goals of American disability rights laws would be reinforced through ratification of the CRPD by the United States, given the stated purpose of the CRPD "to promote, protect and ensure the full and equal enjoyment of all human rights and fundamental freedoms by all persons with disabilities, and to promote respect for their inherent dignity."[87] The next part outlines the CRPD and its relevant articles that are vital for U.S. Government agencies to consider in foreign assistance work.

PART 4. PURSUING DISABILITY-INCLUSIVE DEVELOPMENT THROUGH THE CONVENTION ON THE RIGHTS OF PERSONS WITH DISABILITIES

Introduction

The Convention on the Rights of Persons with Disabilities (CRPD or the Convention),[88] adopted on December 13, 2006, and entered into force on May 3, 2008, is the first legally binding international human rights convention specifically applying human rights to the situation of people with disabilities. It marks a paradigm shift in attitudes and approaches to people with disabilities in international instruments[89] and has been celebrated as the "Declaration of Independence" for people with disabilities worldwide.[90] Notably, the CRPD reflects principles and aims of American disability laws and marks a departure from more traditional medical or charitable models of disability that are still, unfortunately, embedded in many national domestic law and policy frameworks.[91]

Historically, in the United States and throughout the world, people with disabilities were seen as objects in need of medical treatment, pity, social benefits, or rehabilitation, as opposed to claimants of rights capable of living independent, productive lives.[92] The CRPD recognizes that people with disabilities are active agents and holders of rights, thus adopting the social model perspective of disability "as an evolving concept...that...results from the interaction between persons with impairments and attitudinal and environmental barriers that hinders their full and effective participation in society on an equal basis with others" and not as an inherent limitation.[93] To break down these barriers, the Convention utilizes the concept of universal design, which is defined as "the design of products, environments, programmes and services to be usable by all people, to the greatest extent possible, without the need for adaptation or specialized design."[94] The Convention sets forth general principles that inform its overall approach and that apply across the treaty: (1) dignity, individual autonomy including the freedom to make one's own choices, and independence of persons; (2) nondiscrimination, participation, and inclusion in society; (3) respect for difference; (4) equality of opportunity; (5) accessibility; (6) equality between men and women; and (7) respect for the evolving capacities of children with disabilities.[95]

The Convention recognizes that many people with disabilities live in poverty and thus underscores "the critical need to address the negative impact of poverty on persons with disabilities"[96] and acknowledges that many people with disabilities experience multiple forms of discrimination based on economic or other statuses.[97] The CRPD clearly makes nondiscrimination and equal access for people with disabilities a human rights issue and with its enforcement, it has the power to change the way people with disabilities are treated around the world.

The CRPD provides the United States with a tool to promote nondiscrimination and equality for people with disabilities worldwide through its foreign assistance programs. It should also be noted that the United States has signed the CRPD, and while it has not as yet ratified the treaty, its signature does have some important legal implications relevant to the pursuit of disability-inclusive development and the themes outlined in this report.

Implications of Signature and Future Ratification of the CRPD for the United States

The United States signed the CRPD on July 30, 2009.[98] The obligation on a state that has *signed* a treaty but whose consent is *subject to ratification* is clear.[99] In such cases, the signatory state is required *to refrain from acts which would defeat the object and purpose of the treaty.*[100] The signatory state is thus not obligated to comply with all the terms of the treaty, for such a result would render ratification of little purpose or consequence since international legal obligation is clearly triggered and dependent upon ratification (and entry into force).[101] The obligation is to "refrain" from acts that would "defeat" the object and purpose of the treaty. Therefore, the United States, as a signatory state, must not act in a manner that would prevent it from being able to fully comply with the treaty on ratification/entry into force and must refrain from conduct that would invalidate the basic purpose of the treaty. A leading commentator suggests that "[t]he test is objective, and it is not necessary to prove bad faith."[102] The following examples, by no means exhaustive, would surely constitute a breach of the United States' obligations in relation to the CRPD: (1) adoption of policy regarding foreign assistance programming that requires separate programs for people with disabilities or that purports to exclude people with disabilities as beneficiaries; (2) adoption of a law that excludes people with disabilities from voting on the basis of their disability; (3) adoption of a law requiring children with disabilities to be educated in separate schools; (4) funding institutions that segregate people with disabilities from mainstream society; and (5) adoption of a law or policy that strips the autonomy or legal rights of people with disabilities.

The CRPD would enter into force in the United States following ratification. The U.S. Constitution establishes that treaty power is shared between the Executive Branch and the Senate.[103] The President negotiates treaties; however, treaties are also subject to the advice and consent of two-thirds of the Senate.[104] Once a treaty is so approved by the Senate, the President may ratify the treaty.[105] When the President ratifies a treaty, it becomes binding law in all 50 States under the Supremacy Clause.[106]

The existing domestic disability rights legal framework in the United States, combined with its ratification of the CRPD, would send a clear message to the international community that the United States is not only committed, but remains the leader in the global effort to promote disability rights, nondiscrimination, and equality for people with disabilities. The aims and obligations of U.S. disability rights law are consistent with those outlined in the CRPD, including respect for human dignity, nondiscrimination, reasonable accommodation, autonomy, and equal participation.[107] Note that much of the treaty derives from U.S. disability law. The sections below give a more detailed description of the standards set forth in the CRPD and their particular relevance for informing disability-inclusive development within the framework of American foreign assistance programming.

Nondiscrimination and Reasonable Accommodation in the CRPD

The CRPD is the first international human rights convention to explicitly recognize disability as a prohibited ground of discrimination, together with the obligation to ensure that reasonable accommodations are made to facilitate human rights enjoyment by people with disabilities. In so doing, it brings into the international legal framework the core principles of nondiscrimination and equality first introduced into U.S. disability rights law and now reflected in other domestic disability law frameworks, especially through ongoing legal reform as a result of CRPD ratification.

The nondiscrimination and equality provisions in the CRPD are elaborated in Article 5. They require States Parties to ensure the equality of people with disabilities and prohibit any discrimination on the basis of disability.[108] The CRPD defines disability discrimination as "any distinction, exclusion or restriction on the basis of disability" that "has the purpose or effect of impairing or nullifying the recognition, enjoyment or exercise, on an equal basis with others, of all human rights and fundamental freedoms" and it extends to "all forms of discrimination, including denial of reasonable accommodation."[109] Thus, the Convention explicitly recognizes that the failure to provide reasonable accommodation constitutes discrimination. "Reasonable accommodation" under the CRPD is defined as "necessary and appropriate modification and adjustments not imposing a disproportionate or undue burden, where needed in a particular case, to ensure to persons with disabilities the enjoyment or exercise on an equal basis with others of all human rights and fundamental freedoms."[110] Reasonable accommodations must be provided in relation to employment, education, participation in political and public life, and cultural activities, among other areas.

As will be further elaborated below, the nondiscrimination and equality provisions and the duty to provide reasonable accommodation are general obligations and attach to, for example, obligations to make foreign assistance programming inclusive of people with disabilities.

The CRPD on Accessibility

Article 9 of the CRPD lays out clear requirements and standards of accessibility for States Parties to follow in ensuring nondiscrimination and equality for people with disabilities and their full participation in society.[111]

Article 9 is a general obligation and thus applies to all provisions in the CRPD, including those provisions that seek to advance accessible and inclusive international development facilities, programs, and employment opportunities.

Specifically, Article 9 requires states to ensure that people with disabilities are able to access a comprehensive range of venues, facilities, and services on an equal basis with others.[112] Accessibility under the CRPD relates to a wide variety of places and services, such as "buildings, roads, transportation and other indoor and outdoor facilities, including schools, housing, medical facilities, and workplaces," as well as "information and communications" and emergency services.[113] In order to achieve accessibility, Article 9 requires States to identify and eliminate obstacles and barriers to accessibility.[114] The provisions that elaborate the specific measures to be undertaken are quite detailed and attempt to capture the wide range of access needs of people with disabilities in different contexts. They include—

- Developing (and monitoring the implementation of) minimum accessibility standards and guidelines;
- Providing training on accessibility for stakeholders;
- Promoting design, development, production, and distribution of information and communications technologies that address accessibility early in their development and that are provided at minimum cost;
- Promoting access to new information and communications technologies and systems, "including the Internet";
- Providing signage for the public in Braille and other easy-to-read and understand forms;
- Providing live assistance (such as guides, readers, and sign language interpreters); and
- Promoting other "appropriate forms of assistance and support" to ensure access to information.[115]

The scope of Article 9 is not limited to State actors, such as local and national governments, government agencies, and government corporations. Rather, Article 9 implicates private actors, requiring States to "ensure that private entities that offer facilities and services which are open or provided to the public take into account all aspects of accessibility for persons with disabilities."[116] In other words, although the Convention is not directly legally binding on private actors (as only States can be bound by international treaties), it obligates States to ensure that private actors over whom they have control act in a manner consistent with the goals and obligations of Article 9. Although this report focuses on U.S. Government agencies, it is important to note the implications of Article 9 for private U.S. donor organizations and foundations that fund international development programs. The CRPD requires States Parties to "take all appropriate measures to eliminate discrimination on the basis of disability by any person, organization or private enterprise," which applies to Article 9 and all other obligations in the treaty.[117] As an example, the Gates Foundation is a U.S. private foundation that provides extensive funding of international development programs and should ensure its funding is being used to develop accessible facilities and services.[118] Additionally, Article 9's obligation for private entities to ensure accessible premises when they offer services to the public is in line with Title III of the ADA's "public accommodation" requirement.

Accessibility and the CRPD obligations of nondiscrimination and reasonable accommodation act as essential analytical tools in understanding the requirement that States Parties make their international cooperation programs accessible under Article 32. The next section reviews Article 32 and its implications for international development assistance.

Disability and International Development in the CRPD

Article 32 requires States Parties to the Convention to cooperate internationally through partnerships with other States or with relevant international and regional organizations and civil society in support of national measures to give effect to the CRPD.[119] Further, Article 32 makes it clear that all international cooperation efforts, including international development programs, should be accessible and fully inclusive of people with disabilities from design through implementation.[120]

In light of the foregoing, Article 32, together with the articles of general application relevant for the interpretation of Article 32 and specific provisions in the areas of education,[121] employment,[122] living in the community,[123] accessibility,[124] health,[125] and access to justice,[126] among others,[127] have important implications, not only for States Parties and their international donor agencies, but for implementing partners of foreign assistance programs as well. These CRPD provisions provide a framework for international development programs to further advance the rights set forth in the CRPD and to promote best-practice models on inclusive development programming.

As this report primarily focuses on four sectors of overseas programming funded by the United States, the sections that follow highlight provisions of the CRPD that are most relevant to these targeted areas of programming: (1) humanitarian assistance and disaster relief; (2) democracy and governance; (3) economic development; and (4) cultural exchange programs.

Promoting Disability Inclusion in Humanitarian Assistance and Disaster Relief

Failures in ensuring that humanitarian response and assistance to refugees and internally displaced persons take the needs of people with disabilities into account prompted the drafters of the CRPD to include a specific provision on protection in times of risk. The drafters of the CRPD were heavily influenced by the devastating impact of Hurricanes Katrina and Rita and the Asian Tsunami, all of which took place during the course of the CRPD negotiations.[128] To that end, Article 11 of the Convention provides that States Parties take "all necessary measures to ensure the protection and safety of persons with disabilities in situations of risk, including situations of armed conflict, humanitarian emergencies and the occurrence of natural disasters."[129] This provision, combined with Article 32 on ensuring inclusion in international cooperation, including international development and the obligations of nondiscrimination and accessibility, provides the framework for ensuring that humanitarian assistance programs are inclusive of people with disabilities.

Other articles implicitly reference the right of people with disabilities to be included in humanitarian efforts by States Parties. For example, Article 28 compels States Parties to ensure an adequate standard of living and social protection, including equal access to "clean water services" and "public housing programmes."[130] Article 25 requires equal access to health care,[131] while Article 26 makes certain the provision of habilitation and rehabilitation,[132] and Article 20 facilitates access to mobility aids and training.[133] Article 16 of the CRPD requires States Parties to accord protection to people with disabilities from exploitation, violence, and abuse and to provide rehabilitation, reintegration, and protection for survivors of violence and other forms of abuse.[134] These and other provisions provide important standards of protection for people with disabilities who are at risk as a result of natural or man-made disasters.

Promoting Disability Inclusion in Democracy and Governance

The promotion of democratic governance grounded in the Rule of Law is a mainstay of U.S. foreign assistance programming[135] and also engages other major donors internationally. The CRPD provides specific guarantees for people with disabilities to ensure their full participation in political and public life and effective access to justice.

While a number of CRPD provisions are relevant to democracy and governance programming, several merit specific mention: Article 12, on legal capacity, calls on States Parties to take measures to ensure the right of people with disabilities to legal capacity and autonomous decision making.[136] In other words, the provision requires States Parties to ensure that people with disabilities have the right to make their own legal decisions.[137] This includes the right of people with disabilities to own or inherit property, to control their own legal affairs, and to have equal access to mortgages, loans, and other forms of financial credit.[138] In many countries, decision making is swept away for people with disabilities on the basis of discriminatory and procedurally unfair processes. The implications for U.S. Government-funded Rule of Law programming in this context are clear and far-reaching. A commonplace example of these discriminatory processes would be the arbitrary exclusion of people with disabilities in national election laws. Despite pervasive electoral discrimination in many countries, U.S. Government-funded election assessments rarely delve into an often complex legal analysis of disability discrimination in the electoral context. Nor do such assessments specifically identify people with disabilities as beneficiaries of voter education programs and thus fail to ensure voter education materials are accessible to people with various disabilities.[139]

Closely related to the right to make legal decisions is Article 13, on access to justice for people with disabilities.[140] Article 13 guarantees the right of people with disabilities to effective access to justice on an equal basis with others in all phases of the administration of justice, including at preliminary stages, such as initial investigations. It further guarantees the right of people with disabilities to be both direct and indirect participants in the justice system, including participation as witnesses in court proceedings. Article 13 also requires States to provide procedural and age-appropriate accommodations to facilitate access to justice to all people with disabilities. The CRPD also requires States to provide training to those working in the administration of justice in order to help ensure effective access to justice by people with disabilities.

In addition to CRPD provisions that are pertinent to Rule of Law programming, Article 29 on participation in political and public life applies to another core subsector of democracy and governance programming—elections and political processes.[141] Article 29 requires that States Parties take measures to guarantee that people with disabilities have equal access to voting procedures, facilities, and materials as well as equal access to actively participate in the political process.[142] More specifically, people with disabilities have the right to cast their ballot in secret and the right to assistance in order to exercise their right to vote.[143] Beyond voting, people with disabilities have the right to be elected to public office; participate in the conduct of public administration, including the administration of political parties and civil society; and participate in the work of international organizations.[144]

Finally, U.S.-funded democracy and governance programming includes targeted efforts to strengthen civil society and citizen mobilization.[145] In that regard, the CRPD emphasizes the importance of the participation of people with disabilities in all spheres of life, including the development of national and international laws, policies, and programs.[146] The CRPD provisions on international cooperation likewise recognize the role of civil society organizations,[147] as do the national-level monitoring provisions in the CRPD.[148]

The CRPD has specific and concrete applications for inclusive democracy and governance programming. The CRPD framework provides a ready template for inclusion in the full range of U.S. Government-funded democracy and governance work, including the following:

- Justice-sector programs supporting the establishment, rebuilding, or expansion of justice institutions;
- Programs expanding access to legal services;
- Interventions to advance administrative law reform;
- Voter education and observation;
- Awareness raising to increase citizen knowledge of human rights standards; and
- Civil society capacity building.

Ensuring the Inclusion of People with Disabilities in Economic Development

The interrelationship between disability and poverty is captured in the preambular paragraphs of the CRPD and was an impetus for the negotiation of the treaty.[149] Creating equal opportunities for participation in economic life is a core component of the CRPD. The CRPD calls on States Parties in Article 27 to recognize the "right of persons with disabilities to work, on an equal basis with others; this includes the right to the opportunity to gain a living by work freely chosen or accepted in a labour market and work environment that is open, inclusive and accessible to persons with disabilities."[150] Given that U.S.-funded economic development programs are frequently inaccessible, and that microfinance initiatives historically have neglected people with disabilities as potential participants, the CRPD sets forth important obligations for economic development programs.

The CRPD provisions on employment, together with the inclusive development obligations, are significant for economic development assistance.[151] These provisions can and should inform strategic interventions designed and implemented by U.S. Government agencies to ensure that economic development does not increase the equity gap for people with disabilities.

Participation of People with Disabilities in Cultural Exchange

Cultural exchange between the United States and other countries around the world has a long and justifiably proud tradition.[152] Ensuring the participation of both Americans with disabilities and foreigners with disabilities in such programming is essential.

Article 30 of the CRPD recognizes a number of specific measures designed to enhance participation in various realms of social as well as cultural life, calling on States Parties to recognize the right to equal participation in cultural life, including cultural exchange programs[153] The CRPD provides further reinforcement and guidance in relation to cultural exchange programming and its accessibility to people with disabilities, whether for participating Americans or counterparts abroad.

Conclusion

The CRPD, one of the most rapidly ratified human rights treaties ever, is serving as a major impetus for disability inclusion in international development efforts.[154] A handful of donor agencies, in addition to USAID, have committed themselves to disability-inclusive development, and many others are currently formulating policies of inclusion in light of developments in international disability rights.[155] The emergence of disability-inclusive development on the agendas of bilateral and multilateral development donors clearly presents an opportunity for the United States. Fostering implementation of the CRPD through international development programs will allow the United States to broaden and deepen its long-standing commitment to disability inclusion in international development. U.S. ratification of the CRPD would clearly reinforce American leadership in disability rights and support American efforts to press for disability equality around the world.

PART 5. USAID DISABILITY POLICY

Introduction

The National Council on Disability made several recommendations to USAID in 2003 to promote access to and inclusion of people with disabilities in USAID programs. These recommendations included (1) establishing a "Fund for Inclusion"; (2) creating an office on disability in development; and (3) requiring specific action plans to include people with disabilities in strategic planning efforts in all USAID sectors. This part reexamines USAID's Disability Policy, its implementation, and significant developments since 2003 both within USAID and within inclusive development. Further coverage is provided of USAID's Disability Fund and the provision of disability-inclusive development training. The part concludes with research findings concerning the implementation of the Disability Policy, including the identification of areas requiring improvement.

Overview of USAID Disability Policy

The United States Agency for International Development (USAID) is the central U.S. Government agency working to provide assistance to countries recovering from disaster, trying to escape poverty, and engaging in democratic reform.[156] USAID is an independent Federal Government agency that receives foreign policy guidance from the Secretary of State.[157] Its work in five regions supports long-term and equitable economic growth and U.S. foreign policy objectives through programming in agriculture, economic growth and trade, education, health, democracy and governance, and humanitarian assistance.[158]

In 1991, the Government Accountability Office (GAO) undertook an investigation into U.S. foreign assistance programming in developing countries to determine how inclusive they were of people with disabilities.[159] The GAO found, among other things, that while such programs were directly relevant to people with disabilities, disability inclusion remained "sporadic" and concluded that USAID "does not generally attempt to target the people with disabilities in its regular bilateral assistance programs...."[160] Thereafter, in 1996, NCD issued a report entitled *Foreign Policy and Disability*, which reviewed the activities of the U.S. Department of State, USAID, and the U.S. Information Agency and concluded that "the United States does not have a comprehensive foreign policy on disability" and "neither the spirit nor the letter of U.S. disability rights laws is incorporated into the activities of the principal foreign policy agencies."[161]

In 1997, USAID, noting the NCD report and recommendations, issued *USAID Disability Policy Paper*, a nonbinding guidance note.[162] The policy articulated in the 1997 document was grounded in the principle of nondiscrimination, as reflected in U.S. federal disability rights laws, with the objective "[t]o avoid discrimination against people with disabilities in programs which USAID funds and to stimulate an engagement of host country counterparts, governments, implementing organizations and other donors in promoting a climate of nondiscrimination against and equal opportunity for people with disabilities."[163] An additional aim was "to promote the inclusion of people with disabilities both within USAID programs and in host countries where USAID has programs."[164]

The 1996 NCD report was followed by a subsequent NCD review in 2003, *Foreign Policy and Disability: Legislative Strategies and Civil Rights Protections to Ensure Inclusion of People with Disabilities.*[165] In subsequent years, several key developments occurred, particularly within the context of USAID programming. In November 2004, USAID made the 1997 disability guidelines part of USAID policy.[166] The specific objectives of the USAID Disability Policy are as follows:

1) Advance U.S. foreign assistance program goals by promoting the participation and equalization of opportunities of people with disabilities in USAID policy, country and sector strategies, activity designs and implementation;

2) Increase awareness of disability issues within USAID programs and in host countries;

3) Engage other U.S. Government agencies, host-country counterparts, governments, implementing organizations, and other donors in fostering a climate of nondiscrimination against people with disabilities; and

4) Support international advocacy for people with disabilities.[167]

In an effort to deepen its institutional commitment to inclusive development, USAID established two Acquisition and Assistance Policy Directives (AAPDs) in support of implementing the Disability Policy.[168] AAPDs provide information and guidelines for agency personnel and partners involved in the acquisition and assistance process, and these two AAPDs provide agency personnel with information directly applicable to solicitations.[169] AAPD 04-17, *Supporting USAID's Disability Policy in Contracts, Grants, and Cooperative Agreements*,[170] requires USAID contracting officers (COs) and agreement officers (AOs) to include a standard provision in all solicitations and in the resulting awards for contracts, grants, and cooperative agreements. For acquisitions (contracts), COs are required to include the provision "USAID Disability Policy-Acquisition" in Section H of all Requests for Proposals (RFPs).[171] For assistance awards (grants and cooperative agreements), AOs must include the provision "USAID Disability Policy-Assistance" in RFAs and must ensure it is included as a special provision in the award.[172]

The second relevant policy directive issued by USAID, AAPD 05-07, *Supporting USAID's Standards for Accessibility for the Disabled in Contracts, Grants, and Cooperative Agreements*,[173] requires COs and AOs to include a provision that supports USAID's Disability Policy in solicitations by outlining standards for accessibility in all new construction, as well as in renovations of structures, facilities, or buildings. According to this AAPD, the provisions that must be included in all solicitations "set out the agency's objectives regarding disability policy in terms of construction; require compliance with accessibility standards; how to comply in new construction and in alterations to existing structures; and construction related activities that are exempt from the requirements for compliance."[174] For acquisitions, COs must include the provision "Standards for Accessibility for the Disabled in USAID Construction Contracts (September 2004)" in Section H of all RFPs and subsequent contracts.[175] For assistance awards, AOs must include the provision "Standards for Accessibility for the Disabled in USAID Assistance Awards Involving Construction (September 2004)" and must ensure it is included as a special provision in the award.[176]

Although the two policy directives require USAID to include the Disability Policy in all RFAs and RFPs, there are serious limitations that call into question the utility of these provisions and their actual impact on disability inclusion in program implementation. Chief among these concerns are—

1) Examples of solicitations that fail to incorporate the required Disability Policy provision;[177]
2) Placement of the provision at the end of solicitations embedded on a page that offerors and applicants may not closely review;
3) Absence of any requirement that points be allocated for inclusion of people with disabilities in the application-grading process;
4) Lack of any requirement for "statements of work" or "program descriptions" to reference people with disabilities as program participants and beneficiaries; and
5) Absence of any requirement or guidance on budgeting for reasonable accommodations within programming, and thus many programs do not provide reasonable accommodations for people with disabilities to access program materials and activities.[178]

In addition, the second policy directive, *Supporting USAID's Standards for Accessibility for the Disabled in Contracts, Grants, and Cooperative Agreements*, allows USAID to authorize waivers "where compliance with accessibility standards is technically infeasible or presents an undue burden." COs and AOs are required to obtain waivers in accordance with the *USAID Policy on Standards for Accessibility for the Disabled in USAID-Financed Construction*[179] prior to issuing approval. The policy states that "[its] guidance extends the principles of the ADA and the ABA to USAID-financed assistance."[180] Waiver requests "must identify the specific requirements and procedures of the guidelines from which a waiver is sought and provide a detailed explanation, including appropriate information or documentation, as to why a waiver should be granted."[181] In addition to waivers, the policy directive also provides for certain exceptions in construction-related activities.[182] The emergency construction exception applies to structures "intended to be temporary in nature" and, under this exception, emergency construction efforts include providing tents or plastic sheeting, minor repairs, or upgrades to existing structures; rebuilding certain parts of existing structures; or constructing temporary structures.[183] The waivers and exceptions are problematic as they may lead to new construction efforts that are inaccessible and USAID should only authorize such waivers and exceptions in narrowly defined and limited circumstances.

In 2009, the two USAID policy directives were codified in USAID's Automated Directive System (ADS).[184] ADS is USAID's directive management system and thus is crucial to the process of creating binding policy within USAID. USAID policy directives, required procedures, and other guidelines and optional materials are drafted, cleared, and issued through the ADS. The ADS functions as a database of relevant, useful, and valid information that USAID employees need to reference to correctly follow agency directives and guidelines. As AAPDs provide information and guidelines for agency personnel and partners involved in the acquisition and assistance process,[185] AAPD 04- 17 and AAPD 05-07 had to be issued through the ADS. As such, this process codified the two AAPDs, thereby making them binding on all USAID employees.

USAID Reports on the Implementation of the Disability Policy

USAID has issued five reports on the implementation of the USAID Disability Policy, the most recent of which was issued in December 2008.[186] In its *Fifth Report on the Implementation of USAID Disability Policy (Fifth Report)*, USAID set forth the following recommendations to further advance the implementation of its Disability Policy:

1) Increase outreach to and consultation of DPOs and disability leaders by USAID missions, offices, and bureaus;
2) Systematize the inclusion of disability into USAID program selection criteria;
3) Increase formal and nonformal training opportunities and raise awareness of inclusive practices for staff, implementing partners, and DPOs; and
4) Increase the number of missions with disability plans.[187]

The *Fifth Report* illustrates that USAID's commitment to disability inclusion and the uniform implementation of its Disability Policy across all missions is leading to an increase in policies and programs that raise awareness of disability issues and are addressing the needs of people with disabilities. In total, 78 country missions, 8 regional offices, and 13 bureaus and offices voluntarily submitted reports.[188] Missions were more willing to participate in the voluntary disability inclusion reporting process, with 75 percent of missions submitting versus 43 percent for the previous report issued in 2005.[189] The number of missions with disability inclusion plans reached 20 percent, as opposed to "a handful" for the previous report, and 75 percent of respondents reported undertaking programs and activities that benefited people with disabilities.[190] A quarter of the reporting missions indicated an increase in the capacity of local DPOs.[191] The report indicates that the uniform implementation of the USAID Disability Policy has increased the profile of disability inclusion at the mission level. According to the report, it is now standard practice to include the Disability Policy provision in the solicitation process; there is an increasing presence of disability-related programming and program components; missions are disseminating USAID policy information to implementing partners; and missions are seeking greater coordination from experts in the disability field.[192]

Although the *Fifth Report* points to important progress, it does not necessarily follow that the increased percentage of reporting missions resulted from greater implementation of the USAID Disability Policy. This seems especially true considering the percentage of reporting missions (75 percent) compared to reporting missions with disability inclusion plans (20 percent).[193] Missions are not required to have disability-inclusion plans, but it should be noted that missions with inclusion plans are actively advancing the Disability Policy. Furthermore, while all missions were in compliance with equal employment opportunity standards, few missions reported having people with disabilities on staff and fewer still reported making any concerted effort to increase the number of people with disabilities employed by the mission.[194] Additionally, only 10 percent of missions reported collecting any input from people with disabilities.[195] The findings and recommendations provide an important lens through which to review USAID's progress in promoting the Disability Policy agency-wide.

The Disability Fund and Inclusive Development Trainings

In 2005, Congress, under the sponsorship of Sen. Tom Harkin (D-IA), appropriated funds to USAID for "programs and activities to address and protect the rights of people with disabilities in developing countries" through the Consolidated Appropriations Act.[196] The act made funding available for such programs, but also required that USAID establish the Disability Program Fund (hereafter Disability Fund or the Fund), an initiative that supports programs intended to benefit people with disabilities and foster disability inclusion in the development programs supported by USAID.[197] The appropriation was originally $2.5 million,[198] and has grown to approximately $4 million per year and has supported small-scale programs in more than 48 developing countries.[199] The Fund not only supports programs that benefit people with disabilities, but also includes DPOs in project design, implementation, and monitoring and evaluation. The emphasis on partnership with DPOs builds the institutional capacity of DPOs to participate in future USAID and other donor-funded development programs.[200]

In another positive step toward implementation of the USAID Disability Policy, USAID developed an e-training course entitled "Inclusive Development" for staff to learn more about the inclusion of people with disabilities in USAID programs.[201] The e-training course is a learner-controlled course that focuses on ways to include people with disabilities in USAID programs and missions. The course features five online modules: (1) foundations of inclusion; (2) barriers to inclusion; (3) the inclusive development program; (4) leading examples of inclusive development; and (5) inclusive human resources management.[202] The e-training course also consists of self-paced exams to test the learner's knowledge and extensive reference documents for learners to review.[203] At present, the e-training course is voluntary and does not reach as many USAID personnel as it could under a mandatory training directive. While a new incentive has been created according to which mission eligibility to host programs under the Disability Fund requires that at least one mission member must have completed the course, mandatory training would clearly have greater impact. In addition to the voluntary e-training course, USAID has added a disability training component to its new staff training and orientation in Washington, DC.[204] The disability training component was developed in an effort to "[i]ntegrate disability inclusion concepts in other trainings given to new staff" and "to stimulate thinking on the topic and provide specific contact information within the Agency."[205] This marks an important step in the right direction for training

USAID personnel, but has a limited impact as it fails to reach existing USAID employees. A disability training component should be integrated into trainings for all staff members at all levels within USAID. Active learning approaches combined with specific technical tools to help personnel understand how to address disability inclusion within the framework of their specific jobs would deepen knowledge and promote fuller implementation of the USAID Disability Policy.

Appointment of Coordinator on Disability and Inclusive Development

Perhaps one of the more significant developments in USAID's efforts to advance disability-inclusive development in its operations is the appointment in 2010 of a Coordinator on Disability and Inclusive Development. It is premature to provide any assessment of the impact of this appointment on the advancement of USAID's Disability Policy and furtherance of disability-inclusive development. It is clear, however, that the placement of the Coordinator within the Bureau for Policy, Planning and Learning, together with the various initiatives underway to strengthen USAID and the commitment in the QDDR to ensure inclusion in USAID's work, represent unique opportunities to press for much-needed reforms. In order for the Coordinator on Disability and Inclusive Development to realize a much-needed and ambitious agenda, appropriate resources must be allocated for this purpose.

Research Findings on the Implementation of the USAID Disability Policy

The next section reviews the findings from interviews, focus group discussions, and desk-based research on the implementation of the Disability Policy by USAID and provides examples of where the policy is not being adequately implemented, as well as examples that highlight progress toward full implementation of the policy.

Lack of Knowledge Regarding Disability Issues and the USAID Disability Policy

One of the main findings was the serious lack of knowledge that USAID employees have about disability issues and, specifically, *how* to include people with disabilities in development work.[206] Many of the personnel interviewed indicated that they had given little or no thought to the issue of including people with disabilities in USAID programs. Interview participants drew a sharp distinction between programs that include disability components and programs that include gender components and made it clear that gender is far more of a focus of discussion during program design. Further, interviewees indicated that little training is offered on disability issues and even when training sessions are available, few people attend.[207] Few mission personnel who were interviewed knew of any local DPOs in their country or nongovernmental organizations (NGOs) working on disability issues. For those mission employees who indicated they did not know of any DPOs, when asked to describe a DPO, they discussed organizations that provide services to people with disabilities but rarely pointed to organizations composed of people with disabilities.[208] According to the local advocate from Nepal, "their understanding about disability issues is just limited to the health issues, which is one of the major problems among many donor agencies."[209]

USAID personnel interviewed disclosed little awareness of the USAID Disability Policy, or, if they were aware of it, they were unable to articulate its purpose and how it applies to their work.[210] For example, when asked to describe any USAID policy relating to disability of which they were aware, one Program Officer stated, "[t]here is a rule that anything funded with our money must be accessible. So that pertains basically to ramps or removal of barriers. I cannot really recall the exact name of the policy, but it does exist."[211] The officers interviewed in Bangladesh reported there is no disability policy as such "aside from preliminary discussions surrounding an inclusion plan."[212] This is problematic, as the policy cannot effectively impact development programming if it is little known or understood by mission personnel.

A further problem is that some solicitations fail to comply with USAID's solicitation directive, which requires inclusion of the Disability Policy provision in all solicitations. In a review of 66 full solicitations that were issued on the www.grants.gov website from February to July 2010, only 33 of the solicitations included the standard disability provision language outlined in USAID's policy directives.[213] The solicitations issued on www.grants.gov were from missions from around the world as well as from USAID DC.

In reviewing USAID solicitations, there is, however, some evidence of good practice, which should serve as a guide in the effort to see the Disability Policy more uniformly applied throughout the Agency. For example, the West Bank USAID Mission included the required disability provision for new construction efforts in solicitations they released on www.grants.gov during the reviewed period.[214] In addition, the USAID Zambia Mission not only included the Disability Policy provision in its solicitations, but also meaningfully included people with disabilities in statements of work during the reviewed period.[215] This is noteworthy, as Zambia's mission received training on disability-inclusive development funded by USAID.

Disability-Specific Funding Sometimes Reflects Outmoded Approaches
In procurements that fund disability-specific programming, the desk review and interviews disclosed some serious problems in relation to compliance with the letter and spirit of the USAID Disability Policy. Most notably, the U.S. Government's funding of institutions, orphanages, and other segregated settings for people with disabilities—with no apparent attention paid to community-based alternatives or even transition plans—is troubling insofar as these living arrangements do not reflect American or international standards that underscore the importance of living in the community with appropriate supports.[216] To provide one illustration, in a recent RFA from the Republic of Georgia, the mission calls for rebuilding orphanages and specifically mentions children with disabilities as beneficiaries.[217] The proposed project to rebuild Georgia's orphanages is problematic.

American disability law recognizes that living arrangements for people with disabilities must be provided in the least restrictive setting possible and that community living arrangements are preferable to institutional ones.[218] It is often assumed that orphanages offer an acceptable and even desirable place for children with disabilities to live and grow up, whereas it is understood that orphanages tend to segregate children with disabilities from their peers and confine them to an institution, where they are often locked away for the rest of their life. Disability rights organizations have documented the egregious abuses that so often accompany congregate custodial arrangements, including orphanages, and have pointed to the near impossibility of ever providing for the full enjoyment of civil and political rights within institutions, irrespective of the conditions.[219] Investigations into orphanages throughout the world have found that children with disabilities in orphanages do not receive proper education, food, or care, and many are in "deplorable conditions."[220] According to Disability Rights International (DRI), "[o]ne of the main drivers of institutionalization—particularly in developing countries—is the use of misdirected foreign assistance funding to build new institutions or rebuild old crumbling facilities, instead of providing assistance and access to services for families who want to keep their children at home...governments and international donors spend millions worldwide building and rebuilding these torture chambers for children with disabilities instead of supporting families, substitute families when necessary, and community services and education."[221] A staff attorney from DRI interviewed mission personnel in Georgia and discussed the horrific conditions that children with disabilities are often exposed in orphanages in an effort to dissuade the mission from funding the reconstruction. Mission personnel did not change their position on the program and stated that they were funding a program that the local government identified as important and required.[222] This response echoed many of the responses from other mission personnel who claimed they were implementing programs that the local government in the country requested, and yet disability programming should reflect the values and principles of the USAID Disability Policy. The local advocate in Serbia expressed concern over this issue: "Even though USAID is funding projects in Serbia that are recognized by local communities as important and needed, their passivity in reliance on partners which are not critical of the reform and do not possess adequate knowledge, makes them an actor that is *de facto* contributing to exclusion of persons with mental health/intellectual disabilities in Serbia."[223] The local advocate in Nepal expressed similar concerns and noted that mission personnel "did not know about CRPD and explained in plain language they would always focus on what the government of Nepal requests them to do."[224] A core component of any dialogue on disability programming should include principles of nondiscrimination, independence, inputs from people with disabilities, and participation with the local government. Unfortunately, lack of knowledge on the part of USAID mission personnel will constrain such dialogue and limit learning opportunities. The result may well be the funding of inappropriate programming that undermines the USAID Disability Policy, U.S. federal disability law, and the CRPD. This is of considerable concern given that the vast majority of countries around the world possess little to no domestic disability law and policy and those that do, particularly in developing countries, tend to fall well short of the standards applied in either U.S. federal disability law or international disability rights law.[225]

Disability-Specific Programming Favored over Inclusion in General Development Programming

USAID uses a twin-track approach to inclusion by funding small-scale disability-specific programs in addition to promoting its Disability Policy in general development programs. Unfortunately, the disability-specific programs appear to be more effective than the large-scale, general development programs, which disclose very limited disability inclusive development strategies. For example, USAID/Bangladesh has a $90 millionper-year budget, with a single $300,000 grant program for capacity building of DPOs run by Handicap International (HI).[226] When asked about programs that include people with disabilities, the mission personnel stated they did not have any programs that included people with disabilities, but when asked a more specific question they mentioned the disability-specific HI program.[227] This response was similar in interviews at other missions and reveals that missions are not proactively advancing the inclusion of people with disabilities in all programs.[228] USAID's twin-track approach to disability inclusion should systemically build on the successes and lessons learned in disability-specific programs and use such examples as the point of departure for facilitating full inclusion in all USAID programs. When USAID missions implement disability-specific projects, personnel should be trained on how to successfully align those projects with general development programs being implemented at the same time. At issue here is what tools, training, and other strategies could help USAID transition from the twin-track approach to a more comprehensive and holistic approach that fully includes people with disabilities and accords accessibility for all beneficiaries in general development programming.

In the programming reviewed, there were very few general development programs that meaningfully included people with disabilities. Most general development programs had no provisions to include people with disabilities or to provide reasonable accommodations or modifications to facilitate access.[229] USAID personnel in various missions reasoned that there was no need to make accommodations in general development programs, as people with disabilities were not program participants or beneficiaries.[230] The USAID personnel in Egypt reported that only disability-specific programs provide accommodations or modifications for people with disabilities. Further, the USAID personnel interviewed in Armenia stated that "there are no special accommodations made" for people with disabilities to participate in general programming.[231] The interview responses drew a clear line between USAID programs that specifically target people with disabilities versus all other programs, referred to as "general" programs.

Many general programs do not specify disability inclusion at any stage—whether design, implementation, or monitoring and evaluation. On the other hand, programs that are specific to people with disabilities receive a tiny fraction of funding in comparison to general development programs and often only benefit people with specific disabilities, such as programs targeting people who are blind, deaf, or mobility impaired. These programs do not reflect the diversity of disability, and in many cases people with mental health disabilities, intellectual disabilities, or developmental disabilities are completely excluded from such programs. The foregoing suggests that greater attention should be paid to fostering the diversity of disability in USAID programming and to include disability in the broad spectrum of general programming undertaken by USAID. This cannot be accomplished absent specific expertise in disability inclusion across the various sectors of USAID programming.

Monitoring and Evaluation Efforts Fail to Apply a Disability Lens

> Evaluation is the systemic collection and analysis of information about the characteristics and outcomes of programs and projects as a basis for judgments, to improve effectiveness, and/or inform decisions about current or future programming—USAID Evaluation Policy (2011).[232]

The interviews, focus-group discussions, and desk-based research undertaken in the course of the study revealed that very few monitoring and evaluation efforts incorporate a disability lens in development programming. This is problematic as the fundamental purposes of evaluation are "accountability to stakeholders and learning to improve effectiveness." USAID cannot determine whether and how a project effectively included people with disabilities without incorporating a disability lens in monitoring and evaluation efforts. Additionally, monitoring and evaluation efforts that do not include a disability lens have negative implications on budgeting for disability inclusion. The USAID Forward website on "Strengthening Monitoring, Evaluation and Transparency" outlines USAID's new approach to monitoring and evaluation as follows:

> Recognizing that the way in which development programs are monitored and evaluated is inadequate, we will change the Agency's policies, structures and processes that seek to establish USAID as 'best in class' with respect to accountability and learning. To accomplish this goal, we will: 1) Introduce a much-enhanced monitoring and evaluation

process and 2) Link those efforts to our program design, budgeting and strategy work.[233]

Accordingly, it is essential that monitoring and evaluation efforts integrate a disability lens into the monitoring and evaluation framework to ensure that project implementers effectively budget for disability inclusion during project design and report on their use of funds for disability-related project components.

The USAID evaluation policy released in January 2011 fails to mention disability, but the section on gender provides a useful example for how USAID should draft language on disability in evaluations. Gender is listed as one of the basic features that must be included in all evaluations: "gender-sensitive indicators and sex-disaggregated data."[234] The basic feature section of the evaluation policy should use similar language, such as "disability-sensitive indicators."

Many interview and focus-group participants reported that disability is not easy to include in monitoring and evaluation efforts for various reasons. One of the primary issues mentioned focuses on the difficulty of tracking the number of people with disabilities who participate in a project, because not everyone has a visible disability and many people with hidden disabilities may not feel comfortable self-reporting. Although this is important information to consider, this is not at all a sound basis for continuing to exclude disability data in monitoring and evaluation and, in fact, runs counter to international standards, including the CRPD.[235] It is essential that USAID initiate the development of innovative indicators and outputs that have a disability lens but do not require people to self-report on their disability or require USAID and implementing partners to try to determine if someone has a disability. Such an initiative would bring USAID into alignment with international standards on disability data and statistics.

Some good practices warrant mention and can serve as a foundation for further progress in this context. The mission in Vietnam, for example, has proactively included people with disabilities in programs since 1989 and has established useful disability indicators. The personnel interviewed reported that disability-specific indicators and targets had been established and that "the number of persons with disabilities and family members receiving assistance from USAID-funded program is tracked through quarterly and annually performance reports."[236] Likewise, the mission in Ecuador also noted progress in tracking people with disabilities reached in USAID programs.

The monitoring and evaluation efforts that were most effective combined a quantitative and qualitative approach to capturing disability inclusion in projects. The following indicators serve as useful examples for future USAID programming:

- Number of trainings for DPOs
- Number of trainings on disability rights for community members
- Number of DPOs who have participated in program trainings and events
- Number of DPOs with a fund-raising strategic plan
- Number of DPOs that play an important role in awareness-raising activities
- Number of civil society initiatives that include a disability component
- Number of organizations receiving small grants to implement a disability component
- Number of new laws, regulations, or guidelines that are developed

USAID should also promote qualitative methods in monitoring and evaluation efforts that include: detailed document review, case studies, focus groups, project site visits and direct observations, and semistructured key informant interviews.

Disability Rights International's final evaluation from a USAID-funded project in Kosovo provides a useful model for USAID, applicants, and offerors to review in developing monitoring and evaluation efforts during the project design stage that have a disability lens:

> MDRI will survey and monitor participants in all programs to document levels of inclusion and participation by people with mental disabilities before, during, and after the establishment of the program. The survey will document the subjective experiences of program participants, and a monitoring instrument will document the objective outcomes of the project. MDRI will summarize these evaluations and produce a report of lessons learned from this project. The report will include detailed recommendations to civil society and development programs as to how to ensure the effective inclusion of people with mental disabilities in existing programs.[237]

USAID Afghanistan recently issued an RFP that provides a useful example of language for USAID to consider in efforts to promote a disability lens in all monitoring and evaluation efforts. The "Representations and

Instructions" section of the *Stability in Key Areas (SIKA)-West* states, "As part
of the submission the offerors shall provide a proposed Project Monitoring
Plan (PMP) that will include, at a minimum, the following elements and be
capable of generating the following data and reports: Reporting on
disadvantaged groups (Women, Youth, Disabled, etc) with both PMP
indicators and budget/project data."238

Finally, the QDDR places significant emphasis on strengthening USAID's
monitoring and evaluation system by establishing new requirements for
performance evaluations, designing rigorous impact evaluations, linking
evaluations to future funding decisions, and promoting the unbiased appraisal
of programs and the full disclosure of findings.[239] This undertaking, combined
with the commitment in the QDDR to disability inclusion in DOS and USAID
programs, provides a clear mandate for improving the capture of disability-
specific data through the reformed monitoring and evaluation scheme. To this
end, USAID should ensure monitoring and evaluation efforts are conducted
with a disability lens. The recently appointed Coordinator of Disability and
Inclusive Development within the Bureau for Policy, Planning and Learning,
where other efforts to improve data collection are already underway, can
spearhead this process. This effort should be directed at ensuring disability
inclusion in future project design and implementation and the development of
best practices.

Conclusion

The findings relating to USAID and the implementation of its Disability
Policy disclose some positive practices and also support a review of the
Policy, the terms of which were drafted in 1997. A review and revision of the
Policy is timely given the commitment to disability inclusion set forth in the
QDDR and will help facilitate a redoubling of efforts to ensure inclusion in all
programming and to provide specific, concrete, and achievable guidance to
USAID personnel and implementing partners. An emphasis on training that
reaches USAID personnel in Washington, as well as in the missions around
the world, is clearly needed based on the findings. The development of
disability indicators to enrich the monitoring and evaluation of USAID's
programs is likewise timely and warranted. Finally, and presenting a new and
unique challenge, with rapid CRPD ratification occurring across the world, it
becomes ever more important to take disability inclusion into careful account
when designing development assistance programming consonant with local

law and prevailing international standards. Ultimately, taking specific steps to ensure the inclusion of people with disabilities in all foreign assistance programming avoids future human harm and reduces redevelopment costs.

PART 6. USAID SECTOR-SPECIFIC REVIEW

Introduction

In the *Quadrennial Diplomacy and Development Review*, the Obama administration undertook to "rebuild USAID into the world's premier development agency."[240] As discussed in part 5, USAID was one of the first development donors to adopt a policy addressing disability inclusion in foreign assistance programs. In order to keep pace with other donor efforts to advance disability inclusion in development,[241] prompted by domestic as well as international legal developments, USAID needs to redouble its efforts to ensure, pursuant to the QDDR, that disability is fully integrated into the policies and programs of USAID.[242]

The U.S. Government currently prioritizes its development efforts in the following six areas:

1) Food security
2) Global health
3) Global climate change
4) Sustainable economic growth
5) Democracy and governance
6) Humanitarian assistance.[243]

This part focuses on USAID's disability inclusion in three of those sectors: humanitarian assistance, economic development, and democracy and governance. The purpose of this part is to provide a more in-depth analysis combined with salient examples of whether and how disability inclusion occurs in U.S. Government-funded development work. The following sections analyze USAID's disability inclusion within those specific sectors based upon a desk review of key publications, a sampling of USAID-issued solicitations, and key informant interviews with USAID personnel and implementing partners.[244] The part's scope is limited to a review of USAID programs in three sectors, but many of the findings and recommendations set forth are applicable to DOS and other U.S. Government agencies operating overseas.

Additionally, many of the findings and recommendations are relevant to other sectors of international development.

Disaster Relief: Making Humanitarian Preparedness and Response Accessible

The Office of U.S. Foreign Disaster Assistance (OFDA) within USAID facilitates emergency assistance efforts overseas.[245] OFDA's mission is to support humanitarian assistance programs to save lives, relieve human suffering, and diminish the social and economic impact of humanitarian emergencies worldwide.[246] OFDA responds to natural disasters and also provides assistance when lives or livelihoods are threatened by armed conflict, acts of terrorism, or industrial accidents.[247] Additionally, OFDA funds activities to decrease the impact of recurrent natural disasters and supports training to build local capacity for disaster management and response.[248]

According to USAID, "[p]eople with disabilities are substantially more prone to being adversely affected by natural disasters, conflict, or other emergencies, yet they are continually excluded from disaster planning and response efforts."[249] Armed conflict and natural disaster increase the number of people with disabilities by causing injury, impairment, and trauma.[250] Additionally, people with disabilities are disproportionately affected during disaster and armed conflict owing to inaccessible information dissemination, transportation procedures, and overall relief efforts.[251]

OFDA Technical Publications

Desk-based research reviewing USAID's humanitarian assistance programs revealed a dearth of useful information on disability inclusion in USAID policies, guidance documents, and relevant publications directed at OFDA programming. Where people with disabilities are referenced at all, the tendency is to reference their generalized vulnerability without providing any guidance on strategies for ensuring their protection in situations of risk. In this vein, USAID/OFDA's *Guidelines for Unsolicited Proposals and Reporting* includes a short section on disability, stating that "[p]eople with disabilities may become disproportionately vulnerable during times of disaster, due to the disruption of infrastructure, services, and familiar routines."[252] While the publication does acknowledge that proposed interventions should include people with disabilities to the extent possible, it provides no concrete examples or guidelines as to how inclusion can be facilitated, nor does it reference materials that could provide such guidance.[253] Similarly, the *Field Operations Guide (FOG) for Disaster Assessment and Response,* a key reference for field workers undertaking initial assessments and for members of OFDA Disaster Assistance Response Teams (DART), lacks any guidance on disability inclusion.[254] The FOG makes passing reference to disability but fails to provide meaningful instruction for including people with disabilities in assessments. While people with disabilities are identified as a "vulnerable population" that must be targeted for support after a disaster, the FOG does not address how to identify people with disabilities or otherwise point to inclusive strategies. Other technical documents intended to provide guidance in this context similarly fail to provide meaningful direction on disability inclusion.

Likewise, budgeting tools used in the humanitarian assistance context miss opportunities to provide meaningful direction on the implications of disability inclusion and the USAID Disability Policy. The *Sample Detailed Budget for Primary Funding Recipients*, for example, includes a long illustrative list of line items, but does not include a line item for reasonable accommodations for people with disabilities to participate and benefit from programs.[255] In addition to ensuring that technical publications provide relevant guidance on disability inclusion, budgeting references and models should likewise include such references, thereby cuing implementers to the need to account for disability inclusion in costing proposals.

While the focus on disability inclusion in humanitarian assistance in this report is limited to addressing USAID/OFDA, there are indicators of progress in other contexts. InterAction, the umbrella coalition organization of humanitarian assistance organizations, has adopted a section, "Promoting People with Disabilities," into its private voluntary organization (PVO) standards.[256] The standards call for member organizations to establish an internal mechanism to promote and monitor disability inclusion in humanitarian assistance programs[257] and require disability inclusion strategies to be integrated into all programming stages.[258] The PVO standards also state that programs and activities should be held in accessible locations, training and conference materials should be provided in accessible alternate formats, and members should budget for reasonable accommodations for people with disabilities in programs and activities.[259] Notwithstanding these and other efforts to promote disability inclusion, it remains the responsibility of USAID and other U.S. Government agencies to advance disability inclusion in U.S.-funded programming, and these agencies should be setting the standard for nongovernmental humanitarian assistance contractors to follow, certainly not the other way around.

Humanitarian Assistance Sector Conclusion

The foregoing review exposed some significant gaps in disability inclusion within the framework of humanitarian assistance programming and missed opportunities to provide meaningful guidance on inclusion to implementing partners. A concerted effort should be made to ensure that technical publications and budget samples do provide disability-specific guidance on inclusion.

Economic Development: Ensuring the Inclusion of People with Disabilities

The central goals of USAID's economic development programs are to assist developing countries in achieving rapid, sustained, and broad economic growth aimed at ensuring the well-being and livelihoods of their citizens over time.[260] USAID's economic growth strategy, *Securing the Future: A Strategy for Economic Growth*,[261] guides these efforts and comprises three core program approaches: (1) developing well-functioning economies; (2) enhancing access to productive activities; and (3) strengthening the international framework of policies, institutions, and public goods. These core approaches are supported by USAID programming aiming to—

- Improve the environment for enterprise growth and competitiveness;
- Strengthen economic policy and governance;
- Create sound, well-governed financial systems;
- Support business-enabling environments;
- Support microfinance programs and business services for micro and small enterprises; and
- Build trade capacity.[262]

The stated aims of USAID's economic development programming have clear implications for the inclusion of people with disabilities. The International Labor Organization estimates that 386 million of the world's working-age people have disabilities, and unemployment of people with disabilities is as high as 80 percent in some countries.[263] People with disabilities in developing countries make up a disproportionately high level of the world's population living in poverty; thus it is essential that economic development programs be inclusive of people with disabilities. Ensuring disability inclusion and accessibility in USAID's economic development programs is accordingly an important aspect of any successful poverty eradication program. Absent disability inclusion in all subsectors of economic development programming—whether micro-level interventions aimed at income generation or macro-level interventions designed to create economic development-friendly legal and regulatory frameworks—people with disabilities will not be able to fully participate in society. The next section reviews USAID's economic development programming within the context of the USAID Disability Policy.

Economic Development Technical Guidance

Of 20 core technical publications published by USAID concerning economic development, including both technical briefs and publications of USAID's chief economic advisor, none addressed disability inclusion.[264] Even in publications where the disproportionate impact of poverty and joblessness on women was repeatedly referenced and highlighted, no mention was made of people with disabilities and their unique vulnerability, even in the 2009 publication, *A Guide to Economic Growth in Post-Conflict Countries.*[265]

Economic Development Solicitations

This study reviewed numerous economic development solicitations and found that very few solicitations included people with disabilities at all or in any meaningful way. The RFPs reviewed did include the USAID Disability Policy, but failed to list people with disabilities in the statement of work. Further, twelve economic development RFAs were reviewed, but five failed to include the USAID Disability Policy. This is a major issue, as it points to the fact that some Acquisition Officers remain unaware of the policy and fail to include it in RFAs altogether, some seven years after the adoption of the USAID Disability Policy. In RFAs where the policy is included, there were very few that meaningfully mentioned people with disabilities in the program description section. Further, out of six economic development RFPs, only two contained additional information related to people with disabilities in the statement of work.

Examples from USAID Programming

The following examples of USAID economic development programs in countries where interviews were undertaken provide a useful lens through which to review and conceptualize the various types of programs being implemented, as well as whether and how USAID economic development programs are accessible to and inclusive of people with disabilities. The review combines the in-country interview responses that mentioned economic development programs with the desk-based research into economic development programs in the 20 countries included in this study.

In Armenia, the USAID mission supports labor market interventions aimed at providing support to Armenia's jobless population, and the program specifically includes people with disabilities as one of the targeted beneficiary groups.[266] According to Program Officers at the mission, there has been a recent push to include people with disabilities in all programs, and the officers emphasized the importance of including people with disabilities in job-skills workshops.[267]

USAID's "Assistance to Persons with Disabilities" program in Ecuador"[268] supports job placement services and information technology training for people with disabilities to improve their labor profiles.[269] The main objectives of the program are (a) to promote the participation and equalization of opportunities of people with disabilities; (b) to increase awareness of issues of people with disabilities; (c) to engage other U.S. Government agencies, host country governments, implementing organizations, and other donors in fostering a climate of nondiscrimination against people with disabilities; and (d) to support international advocacy for people with disabilities.[270] In 2007, the program trained approximately 1,000 people with disabilities, and 860 found permanent jobs.[271] While this is an example of targeted economic development programming for people with disabilities that has achieved measurable results, the investment for the entire project from 2006 to 2009 was only $766,000.[272] General economic development programming that receives more funding and staff that is accessible to people with disabilities has the potential to benefit even more people with disabilities.

In Egypt, the USAID mission funds a disability-inclusive microfinance program. The mission partners with a microfinance institution that provides loans to people with disabilities and trains them on financial management. There have been more than 3,500 program beneficiaries.

In contrast to the inclusive programs referenced above, USAID Serbia supported a microfinance program, but it did not include people with disabilities. According to an officer at the mission, "we had a microfinance program and handicapped people were not prevented from applying for a loan, for example." This response points to a major misconception in international development programs—the absence of an express prohibition on the participation of people with disabilities does not mean that the program is actually accessible to or inclusive of people with disabilities. The central idea around American federal disability law, and the international standards that have emerged from it, is that disability inclusion requires reasonable accommodation and modification.

Economic Development Sector Conclusion

In reviewing the USAID economic development sector, it is evident that USAID has the capacity and existing framework to create inclusive economic development programming. Deepening efforts at inclusion in this context, including through the provision of technical guidance and more meaningful attempts at highlighting the disability dimension in relevant solicitations, will help narrow equity gaps and eliminate worldwide poverty, advance the goals of USAID's Disability Policy while complying with American disability rights laws, advance the principles of the CRPD, and further prove that the United States is a leader in the inclusive development field.

Democracy and Governance: Achieving the Full Participation of People with Disabilities and Their Representative Organizations in Politics and Public Life

The central goals of USAID's democracy and governance programming include the equal application of the law, transparent and accountable government systems, impartial electoral frameworks, and citizen participation.[273] USAID organizes its democracy and governance work around four core pillars: (1) Rule of Law; (2) Governance; (3) Elections and Political Processes; and (4) Civil Society programming. These programming pillars are essential advocacy entry points for groups subject to discrimination in their societies generally, and for people with disabilities in particular. The fundamental aim of the USAID Disability Policy as applied to these spheres of work is for people with disabilities to be fully included as beneficiaries in any democracy and governance strategy. The following sub-sections review disability inclusion in the four core pillars of USAID democracy and governance programming. Research conducted as part of this sector analysis consisted of a review of democracy and governance solicitations, desk-based research reviewing USAID's Center for Democracy and Governance technical publication series launched in 1998, in-country interviews, and focus-group discussions.

Rule of Law

In the interest of promoting and expanding order and security—essential prerequisites to the Rule of Law—USAID prioritizes the establishment and expansion of justice institutions to ensure the maintenance of public order.[274] Laws must be legitimized in the eyes of the citizenry in order to be successful and lasting. USAID emphasizes the importance of citizen inclusion in legal reform processes, the harmonization of customary law with existing or proposed state-based law, the formation of justice mechanisms to address past abuses, and systems of checks and balances to prevent future abuses.[275] USAID seeks to strengthen rule of law by promoting equal application of the law, protection of human rights and civil liberties, and access to justice for all citizens—especially the poor, people with disabilities, and women.[276]

National disability legal frameworks remain underdeveloped throughout the world, notwithstanding rapid ratification of the CRPD in more than 100 countries. In many countries, domestic law contains blatant discriminatory provisions that seriously undermine access to justice and full participation in society for people with disabilities. The provisions that discriminate against people with disabilities include arbitrary exclusions in electoral codes, sweeping plenary guardianship laws with no due-process protections, discriminatory banking practices, and inaccessible court proceedings. These discriminatory provisions represent a small fraction of the standard practices that USAID should address in general Rule of Law programs. To this end, it is important for Rule of Law programs to include disability-specific technical assistance to promote development of domestic disability laws and policies. Currently, disability-specific guidance is conspicuously absent from technical publications, statements of work, and, consequently, from Rule of Law programming implemented in developing countries.

Governance Programming

Through its governance programming, USAID aims to develop the effectiveness and accountability of government institutions through increasing transparency and universal public participation.[277] By providing technical expertise and leadership—learned and honed through research, trainings, and best practices developed in the field—USAID actively supports country-level governance development programs. USAID prioritizes programs that endeavor to address anticorruption, accountable security-sector systems, the decentralizing and localizing of governance activities, improvements to legislative procedures and processes, democratizing executive branch offices, and the inclusion of democratic structures and precepts into state building.[278]

The inclusion of people with disabilities in governance programming is a necessary precondition to the greater participation of people with disabilities in government. Additionally, the removal of actual or perceived barriers blocking people with disabilities from freely participating in or benefiting from governance programming actualizes USAID's governance-programming mission: "the mere act of governing is not democratic unless the institution and individuals charged with governance...are accessible to everyone."[279]

Elections and Political Processes Programming

USAID election programming assists governments in developing consensus-building practices that promote more inclusive and participatory political processes; election processes that democratically and accurately reflect the will of the people; oversight mechanisms to stifle corruption and ensure that election management bodies operate independently; and multiple political parties that aggregate the interests of different constituencies and ensure that elections are truly contested.[280] Democracy requires free and fair elections occur on a consistent basis and be accessible to all citizens.

People with disabilities have faced many barriers to participation in election programming throughout the world. These programming barriers undermine USAID's strategic focus to promote free and fair elections. Current USAID technical publications on elections and political processes make no mention of people with disabilities. Where programming references people with disabilities as potential beneficiaries, generally no solutions are offered to address the inaccessibility of elections. USAID needs to provide guidance on how to include people with disabilities as beneficiaries of and participants in elections programming so that mission officers are aware of how to design programming that includes and is accessible to the participation and benefit of people with disabilities.

Civil Society Programming

USAID seeks to strengthen the ways in which citizens are freely and openly able to organize and communicate with one another and their government, protections of tolerance and respect for human rights, and the citizenry's capacity to mobilize reform and civic action efforts.[281] Civil society activities help inform public opinion, mobilize voting blocs, and challenge politicians and political parties through policy debate. Often in postconflict countries, civil society organizations lead reconciliation and reconstruction efforts, assisting USAID programming by conducting and commissioning research to improve programs; performing assessments of government programs; managing NGO cooperative agreements; and providing localized and unique technical expertise.[282] The full participation of people with disabilities in civil society is a marker of an open and free society.

Democracy and Governance Technical Guidance in Featured Publications

A review of key democracy and governance publications from the USAID Center for Democracy and Governance and successor publications, intended to provide best practices, lessons learned, and guidelines for practitioner consideration, revealed scant attention to disability inclusion. Further, there were numerous missed opportunities to provide salient guidance to democracy and governance practitioners, even in publications with a "marginalized" population focus or theme. The inclusion of people with disabilities in democracy and governance programming is an essential first step toward the full realization of the rights of people with disabilities; however, USAID program officers and mission staff cannot be expected to understand how best to incorporate people with disabilities into their programming without specific guidance. People with disabilities and disability inclusion are not addressed in the wide range of core democracy and governance publications, whether in Rule of Law,[283] governance (anticorruption,[284] decentralization, policy implementation[285]), elections and political processes,[286] or civil society.[287]

The provision of appropriate guidance on *how* to include people with disabilities as beneficiaries of and participants in all aspects of democracy and governance programming is essential so that mission officers are able to design, implement, and oversee concrete programming that is inclusive of and accessible to people with disabilities.

Democracy and Governance Solicitations

The review considered the meaningful inclusion of people with disabilities in solicitations and their statements of work to assess, for example, whether people with disabilities were referenced as a vulnerable population or potential beneficiaries in relevant program descriptions. While many failed to include people with disabilities or otherwise reference disability inclusion, there are examples of solicitations that did mention people with disabilities. For example, the recently issued *International Rule of Law Technical Assistance Services RFP* listed people with disabilities as program participants in the statement of work and in subsections on the equal application of the law and access to justice.[288]

A recently released RFA from USAID Liberia includes people with disabilities in the program description: "Progress in the Rule of Law sector will continue to be impeded without tangible and large scale efforts to incorporate marginalized groups, including the poor, women, disabled, youth, and those living in rural areas of the country."[289] It also recognizes that "[m]arginalized groups such as the poor and disabled often lack access to the instruments of governance" and that legal literacy outreach programs can provide basic access to justice training and peaceful avenues for recourse.[290] Although the program description meaningfully mentions people with disabilities as beneficiaries, it is noteworthy that this RFA does not include the Disability Policy.[291] USAID Indonesia included people with disabilities in a recently issued Annual Program Statement, noting that "to the extent it can accomplish this goal within the scope of the program objectives; the Recipient should demonstrate a comprehensive and consistent approach for including men, women and children with disabilities."[292]

Democracy and Governance Program Examples

Democracy and governance program examples were elicited from in-country interviews with USAID program officers. The in-country interview questions specifically addressed the four pillars of democracy and governance to determine the level of inclusion and accessibility across the various subsectors:

- The USAID mission in Egypt funds a grant program that is establishing a complaints office to train lawyers on how to draft and file legal complaints. Notably, the grant has been used to train lawyers on the legal rights of people with disabilities, "with a special focus on women."
- USAID Serbia has Rule of Law programming that focuses on judicial reform and the capacity of courts to act independently and transparently. The USAID officer interviewed stated there was no disability-related component in this program and that no trainings included discussion of people with disabilities in the court system.
- USAID Russia worked with Perspektiva, a local disability organization, and its regional partners to develop and implement a training course on advocating the rights of people with disabilities for law students in five Russian universities.
- USAID Vietnam has been proactively including disability components in Rule of Law programs. As part of its disability program, the mission worked with the Vietnam National Assembly to enact the National Disability Law, Vietnam's first comprehensive law for people with disabilities.[293] The mission also worked with various government ministries to address and develop barrier-free codes and standards for public construction and transportation and included training for government officials on the rights of people with disabilities.[294]
- Prior to the last national election in Bangladesh, USAID provided training to DPOs to ensure that polling stations were accessible to people with disabilities and also to inform people with disabilities about their right to cast their vote in secret.[295]
- USAID Serbia has funded election programs, but people with disabilities were not included. According to a Program Officer, "the emphasis was more on professionalizing party systems and strengthening their platforms. In regards to specific groups, we

worked on creation of a coalition of ethnic minorities, but persons with disabilities were not included."

- USAID Serbia is in the final year of the Civil Society Advocacy Initiative, a five-year, $18 million program that includes various disability components. Although this program includes people with disabilities, neither the mission nor the prime implementing partner could provide information about how many people with disabilities participated in program activities. The mission and the prime contractor, the Institute for Sustainable Communities, pointed to the fact that no "disability indicators" were included in the program's monitoring and evaluation plan. This points to the lack of monitoring and evaluation efforts that track people with disabilities discussed in part 5. Large-scale civil society programs must develop indicators in order to monitor and evaluate disability inclusion.

- USAID Indonesia has been proactively including people with disabilities in election programs. Prior to the 2009 general election, the mission worked with the International Foundation for Electoral Systems and the Center for Citizens with Disabilities Access to Election, an Indonesian DPO that focuses on election access for people with disabilities. In this program, USAID supported the development of a voting template for people who are blind or low vision. The template allowed people who are blind or low vision the ability to vote independently at polling stations for the first time in Indonesia and represented a first step toward ensuring the right of all people with disabilities in Indonesia to vote in secret. Additionally, an advocacy toolkit for people with disabilities was developed in consultation with international disability experts, election experts, and DPOs. These activities were part of a much larger election project with a total budget of $3 million.

- Notably, in 2006, USAID funded a two-year project implemented by Disability Rights International, the Initiative for Inclusion of Citizens with Mental Disabilities and their Families in Kosovo, which helped to support one of the most innovative and effective self-advocacy efforts for people with intellectual disabilities and serves as a useful example for future programming. The self-advocacy organization that was established during the project, Ne per Ne (We for Ourselves), has—

- Conducted workshops and panel discussions aimed at policymakers and the public on the rights afforded to all people under the CRPD.
- Opened the doors of Shtime Institution and taken people out to the Ne per Ne meetings and events—people who have spent decades segregated from society and locked behind the doors of the institution.
- Challenged discrimination. After being denied official identification cards in the former Yugoslavia, members of the self-advocacy groups were among the first citizens of Kosovo to receive the new ID cards.
- Held a candidate's question-and-answer forum during the political campaign season during Kosovo's first election as an independent state, allowing persons with intellectual disabilities to vote for the first time.
- Published *Success Stories*, a book of personal narratives describing the experience of disability in Kosovo and how lives have been transformed through self-advocacy. The book is now part of the curriculum of middle and high schools throughout Kosovo.
- Established an internship program with the University of Prishtina that introduces for all psychology students a required internship placement with the self-advocacy group.
- Lectured at schools and the university and conducted television and newspaper interviews as part of their advocacy effort for inclusive education and to break down barriers and reduce the stigma and discrimination against people with intellectual disabilities.

Democracy and Governance Sector Conclusion

The foregoing review reveals some good examples of inclusive programming in the democracy and governance sector but also reveals numerous missed opportunities to provide important guidance on disability inclusion, even in areas where USAID has considerable good practice, as in election access. USAID's Democracy and Governance Technical Publication Series, an excellent resource for democracy and governance practitioners, has not been used to forward the USAID Disability Policy, either through disability-specific publications or through disability inclusion in key publications. Moreover, USAID solicitations routinely fail to capture even the most rudimentary opportunities to advance disability inclusion in statements of work, often missing people with disabilities as specifically identified beneficiaries in programs targeting the most vulnerable groups in society. Achieving the aims of the QDDR to ensure full inclusion in USAID democracy and governance programming will therefore require changes that provide democracy and governance practitioners, whether USAID personnel or its implementing partners, with disability-specific best practices, lessons learned and guidelines, and a more nuanced approach to inclusion in statements of work and solicitations generally.

PART 7. REVIEW OF DEPARTMENT OF STATE: COUNTRY REPORTS ON HUMAN RIGHTS, EMBASSY ACCESSIBILITY, AND CULTURAL EXCHANGE PROGRAMS

The U.S. Department of State (DOS) is the government agency responsible for foreign diplomacy.[296] The head of DOS, the Secretary of State, is the President's lead foreign policy advisor. The agency's mission is to "[a]dvance freedom for the benefit of the American people and the international community by helping to build and sustain a more democratic, secure, and prosperous world composed of well-governed states that respond to the needs of their people, reduce widespread poverty, and act responsibly within the international system."[297]

The current priorities for DOS are to protect the United States and its citizens; promote democracy and human rights; protect and promote U.S. interests, values, and policies; and support all of those in the field implementing the foreign policy initiatives that help make these other goals a reality.[298] More concretely, DOS day-to-day duties include managing all U.S. embassies and consular offices in foreign countries, negotiating treaties and agreements on issues ranging from trade to weaponry, organizing the international activities of other departments and hosting official visits, and managing the U.S. foreign relations budget.[299] Of particular relevance for the purposes of this report are the roles that DOS plays in monitoring country human rights conditions through its Bureau of Democracy, Human Rights and Labor (DRL). Also, DOS oversees embassy and mission accessibility and implementation of cultural exchange programs, most notably those of the Bureau of Educational and Cultural Affairs.

In June 2010, the Obama administration created a new position within DRL to further its commitment to supporting the CRPD, the Special Advisor on International Disability Rights.[300] The purpose of the Special Advisor is to "include issues affecting people with disabilities across the world in all aspects of [DOS] work."[301] The National Council on Disability commends this appointment and recommends that DOS provide adequate resources in order to achieve the objectives of that office.

The sections that follow address disability inclusion within the context of the DOS Country Reports on Human Rights, embassy accessibility (premises and information), and accessibility of cultural exchange programs funded by DOS.

Country Reports on Human Rights

The Office of Democracy, Human Rights, and Labor (DRL) within DOS submits Country Reports on Human Rights Practices annually to Congress in compliance with sections 116(d) and 502B(b) of the Foreign Assistance Act of 1961, as amended, and section 504 of the Trade Act of 1974, as amended.[302] These laws require the Secretary of State to provide to the Speaker of the House of Representatives and the Committee on Foreign Relations of the Senate "a full and complete report regarding the status of internationally recognized human rights, within the meaning of subsection (A) in countries that receive assistance under this part, and (B) in all other foreign countries which are members of the United Nations and which are not otherwise the subject of a human rights report under this Act."[303] According to DRL, "[t]he reports cover internationally recognized individual, civil, political, and worker rights, as set forth in the Universal Declaration of Human Rights,"[304] and consist of some 5,000 pages on human rights conditions in more than 190 countries that is respected globally for its objectivity and accuracy."[305] Critically, for people seeking asylum, DRL also provides relevant information on country conditions to the Immigration and Naturalization Service and immigration judges in asylum cases.[306]

In 2003, NCD recommended that Congress require DOS to document human rights violations against people with disabilities in the Country Reports.[307] In follow-up, this study reviewed the 194 Country Reports on Human Rights from 2009 to determine whether and how violations were documented. Information on disability can be found under Section 6: Discrimination, Societal Abuses, and Trafficking in Persons in these reports, within a subsection entitled "Persons with Disabilities," usually following subsections on "Women and Children."[308] Of the 194 reports, all except Western Sahara include the "Persons with Disabilities" subsection.[309] The introduction to Section 6 provides an overview as to whether certain populations are protected by law and states generally, and whether these laws are enforced or not, sometimes with references to people with disabilities.[310] In addition, each Country Report begins with a summary introduction to the full report, which may or may not mention people with disabilities.[311]

In-Depth Review of Reports

The disability subsections in the Country Reports on Human Rights Practices reviewed for the purposes of this report ranged widely in scope, specificity, and length. Some were cast in very general terms and were therefore of little utility.[312] Other reports used government information or other data to provide statistics on the status of people with disabilities in employment, education, health care, and other spheres.[313] Statistics about people with disabilities in the legal system were informative,[314] and information about government agencies responsible for disability issues[315] improved the usefulness of the report. The more informative reports provided illustrations of specific human rights violations and actions to prevent such violations in the future.[316] There was a correlation between the number of sources referenced in the report, including media sources, government sources, DPOs, and NGOs, and the depth and development of the report.[317]

In order to perform a more complete analysis of the overall breadth of the 2009 reports, the inclusion of information from nine categories was examined for each country: (1) concrete statistics on employment, education, and health care; (2) the rights of workers with disabilities; (3) laws that prohibit discrimination or require accommodations for people with disabilities; (4) specific government agencies or departments; (5) specific international and domestic NGOs and DPOs; (6) specific examples of human rights violations; (7) political/civic participation; (8) additional information on women or children with disabilities; and (9) additional information located outside the "Persons with Disabilities" subsection. The number of country reports that contained information from each category was recorded and calculated as a percentage of total country reports.

National Council on Disability

The review does not evaluate each country's human rights record; it simply assesses the inclusion of information in the reports.[318] For example, although 98.5 percent of the country reports mention *whether* there are laws regarding discrimination against people with disabilities, not every country in this group has or enforces such laws. The table below illustrates the review with a description of each category and the percentage of total country reports that include information from these categories.

Category	Description of Category	% of Country Reports That Include Information from Category
Concrete statistics on employment, education, and health care	N/A	23.20%
The rights of workers with disabilities	Policies that require a certain percentage of employees with disabilities. Also includes the mention of any discrimination against employees with disabilities. Some reports included information on workers with disabilities in Section 7, Workers' Rights.	22.70%
Laws that prohibit discrimination or require accommodations for people with disabilities	Whether laws exist that prohibit discrimination against people with disabilities and/or require reasonable accommodations for people with disabilities.	98.50%
Specific government agencies or departments	Identifies specific departments, agencies, or ministries that provide services to people with disabilities, or provide support to DPOs and NGOs that work with people with disabilities.	67.50%
Specific international and domestic DPOs and NGOs	Discusses specific DPOs and NGOs that advocate for the rights of people with disabilities; provide aid, funding, and services to people with disabilities; or conduct research on human rights violations against people with disabilities.	34.50%
Specific examples of human rights violations	Discusses specific and individual examples of human rights violations against people with disabilities (e.g., provides names of victims, specific dates, locations, and the type of discrimination).	13.90%

Category	Description of Category	% of Country Reports That Include Information from Category
Political/civic participation	Election access for people with disabilities. This category includes reports that discuss access to polling places and voting ballots for people with disabilities. It also includes reports that mention congressional/parliamentary quotas (positions that are designated for people with disabilities).	10.80%
Additional information on women or children with disabilities	Reports that specifically mention the status of women or children with disabilities. This information could be found either under the "Persons with Disabilities" section or elsewhere in the report.	20.10%
Additional information located outside "Persons with Disabilities" section	This category is included to show the number of country reports that mention disability issues in other sections. The sections that are most likely to include such information are Section 5, Governmental Attitude Regarding International and Nongovernmental Investigation of Alleged Violations of Human Rights, Section 2, Respect for Civil Liberties, Section 1, Respect for the Integrity of the Person, and Section 7, Workers' Rights.	24.70%

Selected Country Analysis

The following are summaries of both good models for reporting on the human rights of people with disabilities and examples of human rights reporting on people with disabilities that could be improved through deeper research garnering detail from additional sources; going into greater detail and depth; and eliciting information directly from in-country DPOs or international organizations working in country or having knowledge of the local disability community.

In Ghana, the Country Report drew on different sources to give a complete and illustrative picture of discrimination against people with disabilities.[319] The report drew from news sources, government agencies,

NGOs, and disability and human rights activists.[320] It highlighted the mechanisms of Ghana's legal system through mentioning the role of its constitution, courts, and legislature.[321] In addition, the report drew attention to both societal/religious views on disability and specific cases of abuse and disability discrimination.[322]

Uganda also provides a useful example of detailed reporting, as the Country Report critically and thoroughly evaluated human rights violations against people with disabilities.[323] The report noted that while legislation prohibits discrimination and protects people with disabilities, the law was seldom enforced.[324] The report also noted that several complaints had been filed with the Uganda Human Rights Commission and described specific cases of discrimination and action taken to eliminate discrimination against people with disabilities.[325] Notably, the embassy communicated with DPOs to create the report and also researched the role of several government agencies, which enhanced the coverage.[326]

The embassy in Russia, likewise, undertook a detailed review in its reporting on people with disabilities. The Country Report for Russia was well documented and included population statistics, news sources, and material from government agencies, DPOs, and NGOs.[327] It also included a detailed analysis of disability law (or lack thereof) in Russia, including building accessibility, voting, education, and employment.[328] Further, the report highlighted failed mechanisms of preventing discrimination in access to employment and education and procedures for contesting institutionalization.[329] Significantly, the links between the embassy and USAID mission in Russia to disability groups are strong, suggesting a correlation between engagements with DPOs and detailed reporting.

The Country Report for Armenia provided more detailed coverage of disability issues than other reports. Notably, the Armenian report was one of the very few to specifically reference people with disabilities in its introductory summary.[330] Sources for the report varied, including material from NGOs, government agencies, and news sources, disclosing a depth of research that few of the reports matched.[331] The report documented specific instances of discrimination and abuse against people with disabilities.[332] It also addressed shortcomings in implementation: While Armenian law prohibits discrimination against people with disabilities in employment, education, access to health care, building access, and other services, discrimination still remained a significant problem.[333]

The 2009 Country Human Rights Report for India also served as a useful example of detailed reporting on the human rights situation of people with disabilities. The report used a variety of sources, including information from NGOs, government agencies, statistics from the World Bank, universities, news sources, and relevant disability law.[334] The report also cited information disclosing government action plans to combat discrimination in employment and education and also provided details on different projects and resources implemented by agencies, DPOs, and NGOs.[335]

While the above represent examples of disability rights reporting that clearly meet human rights reporting standards, other reports fall below these standards and are, in some instances, of little value. Thus, in Namibia, while the embassy's report did reference the previous year's report, the report only mentioned the role of one government agency and included mostly generalized statements.[336] More depth into legal mechanisms of action and specific examples of discrimination would be helpful. Similarly, Zambia's 2009 Country Report was extremely brief and provided little useful information on the status of people with disabilities.[337] The report only referenced one news source and one government agency.[338] The embassy did not reach out to local DPOs and thus did not properly address the human rights of people with disabilities in its research.[339] This is surprising given that Zambia's umbrella DPO coalition, the Zambian Federation of Persons with Disabilities, is very well known to USAID and other donors for its work in the area of disability inclusion in HIV/AIDS programming and for its active role in ensuring that the new Zambian Constitution explicitly references disability as a prohibited ground of discrimination, among other disability rights advocacy efforts.

The sparseness of the disability section in Nepal's 2009 Country Report was even more remarkable, consisting of only one paragraph.[340] Brief mention was given to the lack of disability laws and enforcement of law to prevent discrimination in employment, education, health care, and access to other state services.[341] No coverage was provided of the ongoing efforts of the local disability community to establish independent living centers and engage in national law reform, nor was any attention given to the well-known efforts on the part of the disability community to engage in the constitution drafting process. More specific examples of discrimination, an in-depth review of disability law, and the use of additional sources would very likely have uncovered some of these details and made for a more enlightening read.

A final illustration underscoring the limitations of scant disability rights coverage is the Colombian 2009 Country Report.[342] The "Persons with Disabilities" section only mentioned the government agency designated to protect the rights of people with disabilities and that some disability law preventing discrimination existed.[343] There was no mention of communication with DPOs or NGOs.[344] It stands to reason that communication between the Human Rights Officer at the embassy and the democracy and governance staff at USAID might foster the kind of information flow that is essential to meaningful human rights reporting.

In reviewing the level of detail and information provided in the various reports, it is clear that embassy officials should use the resources available to them. In particular, they should be encouraged to reach out to local DPOs and international disability organizations to ensure that the situation of people with disabilities is accurately reflected and included in these reports.[345] Many Human Rights Officers reported being unaware of any DPOs in the country in which they worked and therefore did not consult with a DPO while drafting the report.[346] To be sure, Human Rights Officers cannot be expected to possess expert, in-depth knowledge of all human rights matters in the country in which they work. They can, however, adhere to best practices in human rights reporting in the areas they do cover and achieve a baseline of quality reporting for those human rights issues. Ensuring disability rights training and materials in Human Rights Officer development is one approach that could, over time, make quality disability rights reporting the norm in all country human rights reports.

Embassy Accessibility

Local advocates conducted interviews and assessments in 14 U.S. embassies in developing countries to determine the accessibility of the facilities, programs, and employment opportunities administered by the embassy for people with disabilities.

Security Concerns Trump Accessibility

The main finding from the site visits by local advocates was that security concerns trumped accessibility for people with disabilities. Repeatedly, as local advocates identified accessibility issues with embassy officials, embassy officials responded by citing security as the main reason a facility or service was not accessible. Interview responses disclosed no case in which discussion about how accessibility for people with disabilities could be achieved within the framework of ensuring the security of facilities and information. One prominent example reported in many of the in-country interviews described the inoperability of push-button doors—which accommodate people who use wheelchairs and other people with mobility disabilities—in embassies or missions as a result of security concerns. Local advocates noted that there were electronic push buttons for many entranceway doors, but in many instances those push buttons were turned off due to "security concerns" that the door might open on its own after the button was pushed. The concerns cited did not offer reasoning or actual data concerning threats to security, but rather highlighted the fact that security trumps accessibility.

Security concerns were also cited as the reason that certain materials on websites remain inaccessible. The main websites for embassies were all accessible for screen-reading technology used by people who are blind, have low vision, or have print disabilities, but certain information and materials that were links off the main page were not accessible. Embassy officials noted that some documents had to be "locked," making them inaccessible to screen-reading technology, for security purposes. The embassy officials did not purport to have a great deal of knowledge about "open-source" documents that are accessible to screen-readers versus "locked" documents, but they did believe that documents were locked owing to security concerns (e.g., because it is easier to replicate information from open-source documents, thus it is easier to alter information on important forms, such as visa applications, if the document is open-sourced). This is another example of security concerns trumping accessibility and points to the fact that DOS and other U.S. Government agencies need to ensure accessibility for people with disabilities and reconcile this issue with security measures.

Information and Materials Are Not Provided in Accessible Formats

Taking appropriate measures to ensure that people with disabilities enjoy equal access to information and communications, including information and communication technologies and systems, is surely part of effective diplomacy, development, and conflict prevention and resolution. The provision of information and services in accessible and usable formats for people with disabilities is one area where, in response to the query of the Secretary of State in the QDDR ("How can we do better?"),[347] DOS can and should do better.

A key finding resulting from the in-country assessments was that embassies are not providing information and materials in accessible formats to people with disabilities with any degree of consistency. There are various manifestations of this shortcoming. The majority of embassy assessments found that U.S. embassies do not provide sign language interpreters for visa applicants. In Zambia, the embassy noted that it does not provide sign language interpreters on the basis that language interpreters are not provided to visa applicants. Follow-up questions regarding this issue revealed that embassy officials may not have an awareness of the distinction between providing language interpreters for people who do not speak English and sign language interpreters as an accommodation for applicants with disabilities. Further, not every embassy assessed provides visa applications in an accessible format to people who are blind, have low vision, or have print disabilities. While paper visa applications are still standard in many embassies, there is a shift toward electronic applications. The embassy officials interviewed could not answer questions about the accessibility of electronic visa applications, but they all expressed interest in making sure those documents are provided in an accessible format online. More must be done to address the prevalence of PDF documents, as these are very difficult for persons who use screen-reading technology to access.

With specific regard to website accessibility, all of the main embassy websites reviewed as part of the assessment were accessible to screen-reading technology; however, not all of the links from the main website were accessible to various screen readers.[348] Further, many embassy websites failed to list TTY (teletypewriter) numbers for people who are deaf and who use this technology.

The local advocate in Nepal drafted a detailed and informative summary of the embassy assessment that reflects many of the issues that were pointed out in other embassy assessments:

> The U.S. Embassy and USAID are in the same building. The building, constructed in 2007, is on the same level which allows access to wheelchair users, but, although they claim they follow the ADA completely, we could not find any consideration for visually impaired persons, like tactile block, signage size, text design, color and contrast, sign positioning, handrail texture, railings, lighting and switches to find the way, the use of colors combination in the interior design. There was not any sound system in the elevator and the elevator did not make it possible for a wheelchair user to get out without turning the chair. The toilet is accessible to wheelchair users, but the level of washbasin and urinals is too high for wheelchair users. There was a small library for the general public, but we could not find any materials for visually impaired

people (but they show interest to add material for visually impaired people). We could not find any system, programs or even the future plan to address the issues in accessibility for other kind of disability like people who are deaf or hearing impaired, intellectual disability, blind and physical disabilities. Most interestingly when we asked to show the VISA interview section to assess whether the sill height of the VISA interview window is suitable for wheelchair users or not, they did not show any interest to address our request although the visa section is open to the general public.[349]

The advocate in Armenia noted that the embassy was fairly accessible to people who use wheelchairs but expressed other accessibility concerns similar to those raised in the Nepal assessment: "[T]here were no specific facilities for people who are deaf or blind. We did not notice any yellow signs, no voice commands in elevators." The local advocate in Colombia was allowed to view the visa interview window and noted that it was not accessible to people who use wheelchairs. He also noted that while the visa office does have an accessible window (placed at a height reachable for a wheelchair user), it was not being used for this purpose: It was serving as a bookcase. This issue was brought to the attention of embassy officials and they immediately opened the window for visa interviews.

Cultural Exchanges: Ensuring Inclusion of People with Disabilities in the Design and Implementation of Cultural Exchange Programs

The United States has a long and justifiably proud history of facilitating cultural exchange programs around the world.[350] Indeed, for more than half a century the United States has supported a wide variety of international educational and cultural exchange programs to enhance cross-cultural understanding and to build bridges between communities as a means of peace-building.[351] These programs take many forms and have been particularly successful in bringing future leaders from around the world to the United States to experience the American educational system, enhance their knowledge in major fields of study, and explore American culture and values.[352] At the same time, cultural exchange programs provide Americans with invaluable experiences and insight from other countries.[353] The cultural exchange programs funded by the U.S. Government are extensive and far-reaching and, in line with the stated objectives of the Obama Administration, are likely to be incrementally increased over time.[354] As such, it is vital that cultural exchange programs be accessible to and inclusive of people with disabilities.

Various educational and cultural exchange programs are sponsored and operated through U.S. embassies abroad, many in partnership with governmental and nongovernmental institutions. These include the variety of exchanges falling within the J-1 Private Programs and include programs to the United States, such as au pair programs, internships, and summer/work and travel programs.[355] In addition, there are a variety of academic exchange programs, which differ by region, embassy, and supporting organization. The DOS Bureau of Educational and Cultural Affairs funds several prestigious exchange programs (Fulbright, Humphrey, State, and Muskie)[356] that are offered out of nearly every U.S. embassy in the world.

The Fulbright Program, a prestigious grant program for international educational exchange for scholars, educators, graduate students, and professionals,[357] is an example of a cultural exchange program that has developed policies to include people with disabilities.[358] The program includes staff training on the inclusion of people with disabilities in cultural exchange programs, and uses the resources and manuals from Mobility International USA (MIUSA), an organization specializing in international exchange programs for people with disabilities.[359] Training resources from MIUSA include recruitment materials,[360] participant advising,[361] overseas placement,[362] and general suggestions[363] for including students with disabilities in exchange programs. The Fulbright Program also refers people to a MIUSA-administered webinar on inclusive cultural exchange programs that is funded by DOS.[364] Additionally, Fulbright applicants are subject to the Mutual Educational and Cultural Exchange Act of 1961,[365] which prohibits discrimination on the basis of disability.[366] The Fulbright Program is a good example of a cultural exchange program that is accessible to and inclusive of people with disabilities, and DOS should be commended for its implementation and encouraged to ensure that all cultural exchange programs run out of embassies are accessible to people with disabilities.

In addition to the aforementioned cultural exchange programs, DOS funds a MIUSA program to implement high school exchange programs for students with disabilities.

These programs work with international high school students with disabilities on developing their advocacy skills and assist with their transition to living in the United States.[367] These programs not only help to prepare students with disabilities to benefit the most from DOS-funded cultural exchange programs, but they also provide an important guiding practice for the inclusion of students with disabilities in exchange programs.

Conclusion

The foregoing findings reveal some considerable progress in embassy accessibility, in disability inclusion in the context of cultural exchange programs funded by DOS, and in the coverage of the human rights of people with disabilities in the DOS Country Human Rights Reports. At the same time, the review revealed gaps and areas where more progress can and should be made, particularly in light of the strong commitment to inclusion of people with disabilities reflected in the QDDR.

The DOS Country Human Rights Reports have strengthened their coverage of disability human rights issues. Still, there is considerable room for improvement as coverage remains inconsistent across the Reports. Providing Human Rights Officers with a user-friendly basic template that tracks key components of the CRPD coupled with improved training on disability human rights issues would no doubt help standardize reporting. The recent appointment of a Disability Human Rights Advisor at DOS provides an opportune time for review and revisions to improve current practice.

Incremental improvements in embassy and mission accessibility are readily apparent, and yet the review revealed remaining gaps that require attention. These include ensuring that embassy services and information are readily accessible to persons with disabilities. In addition, there must be continued review of security measures with the aim of introducing measures that mitigate barriers.

In the context of cultural exchange and with the aim of ensuring that programs funded by DOS are made accessible, DOS should support trainings for staff of cultural exchange programs on the inclusion of people with disabilities. The adoption of specific disability-inclusive mission statements and policies that encourage qualified people with disabilities to apply would likely attract greater participation. Improvements should be made to ensure that all information on programs is in accessible alternative formats (website materials, print, and in person) and that accessible housing options are available, along with individualized accommodations.

PART 8. U.S. DEPARTMENT OF DEFENSE: A REVIEW OF OVERSEAS BUILDING AND INFRASTRUCTURE EFFORTS

Traditionally, U.S. civilian government agencies, such as DOS and USAID, have dominated the development sector abroad. However, in recent years, the Department of Defense (DOD) has played a more significant role in capacity and infrastructure building in developing countries.[368] From 2002 to 2005, the Pentagon's budget for official development assistance (ODA) increased from 5.6 percent to 21.7 percent.[369] DOD now accounts for more than 20 percent of U.S. ODA.[370] Examples of DOD ODA projects include the Iraqi Relief and Reconstruction Fund,[371] the Tsunami Relief and Reconstruction Funds,[372] the Global HIV/AIDS initiative,[373]; and Overseas Humanitarian, Disaster, and Civic Aid (OHDACA).[374] DOD also supports other humanitarian aid-related programming outside of ODA through counterterrorism and capacity-building commands such as the Africa Command (AFRICOM).[375] Therefore, it is extremely important to review DOD accessibility standards and practices to ensure that new U.S.-funded infrastructure efforts are accessible to people with disabilities.

The part reviews DOD-funded infrastructure efforts and policies to determine the accessibility of newly constructed buildings, transportation systems, information systems, and other forms of infrastructure for people with disabilities. It is essential that newly constructed, DOD-funded infrastructure be accessible beginning with the design stages. When newly constructed infrastructure is built in an accessible manner, it sets a standard in the country for future projects. Additionally, when physical infrastructure is made accessible from the beginning, DOD and other U.S. agencies avoid substantial future costs associated with retrofitting. Accordingly, it is imperative that DOD adhere to accessibility standards and support the building of accessible infrastructure in postconflict and developing countries.

In December 2008, DOD adopted new accessibility standards under the Architectural Barriers Act of 1968 (ABA) for all DOD-funded construction projects.[376] These standards define the requirements that must be "applied during the design, construction, additions to, and alteration of sites, facilities, buildings, and elements to the extent required by regulations issued by federal agencies under the ADA of 1990."[377] The purpose of the new standards is to ensure that newly constructed facilities are accessible to people with disabilities.[378] Although the standards generally apply to international projects, many overseas projects fall under an exemption and therefore are excluded.

For example, "[f]acilities in other countries for which the United States contributes a portion of the construction cost but does not control design criteria (such as NATO-funded facilities) need not comply with these standards,"[379] but the exception goes on to state that "accessibility is recommended if obtainable."[380] Another exception states, "[f]acilities leased by the United States in other countries need not be accessible pursuant to U.S. law."[381]

Facility accessibility exceptions laid out in DOD policy memoranda are problematic for various reasons. In programs where the United States is a contributing funder but does not control the design criteria, the language "accessibility is recommended if obtainable" is unlikely to yield accessibility gains. If DOD or any other U.S. agency is contributing funds to new infrastructure, the language should not allow for voluntary compliance, but must require accessibility and, in light of rapid CRPD ratification worldwide, compliance with accessibility standards should be the norm. Further, if a U.S. Government agency is leasing buildings in another country, such buildings should be accessible, or easily made accessible, so that Americans and locals with disabilities can enjoy ready access to the building. Allowing DOD to comply with host country accessibility laws is also unacceptable because many host countries do not have accessibility laws or guidelines and the ones that do are often lacking in comparison to American accessibility laws and policies. For the United States to remain a leader in accessibility standards and their adherence, DOD should adhere to American accessibility standards for its overseas facilities.

As ratification of the CRPD continues at a rapid pace, the inconsistencies in accessibility guidelines should lessen as ratifying countries adopt accessibility laws at the domestic level in line with the CRPD. However, in countries that have not ratified the CRPD, DOD's policy of compliance with host country laws creates inconsistency in regional accessibility standards. Moreover, given the underdeveloped state of disability law frameworks, adhering to local accessibility standards often means ignoring accessibility altogether.

A further problem in this context is the permissible derogation from accessibility standards during times of emergency. Section F202.6 of the *ABA Accessibility Standard for DOD Facilities* applies to Federal Government leases and requires that leased buildings or new facilities comply with the ABA guidelines. However, "Buildings or facilities leased for use by officials servicing disasters on a temporary, emergency basis shall not be required to comply with F202.6."[382] This loophole allows DOD contractors to avoid accessibility during times of temporary emergency or disaster response. Given the vast amount of ODA being apportioned to DOD for implementation, this gaping loophole sets an unacceptable standard of discrimination in times of emergency.

Conclusion

The foregoing review highlights the far-reaching implications of DOD-funded overseas building and infrastructure, a woefully understudied issue that is seriously in need of further research. The findings suggest that DOD waivers are undermining accessibility at the expense of inclusion and without justification. DOD should work to limit the number of waivers and exceptions permitted under its newly adopted ABA *Accessibility Standards for DOD Facilities*. In addition, DOD should review waivers and exceptions before authorizing them to ensure that they are used only in narrowly defined circumstances and only where necessary. DOD should also provide clear guidance to contractors on the appropriate application of the ABA Accessibility Standards in postconflict and developing countries and work to close the gap that allows contractors to apply for waivers or argue for an exception overseas. These standards must clearly indicate that DOD infrastructure projects in postconflict and developing countries are subject to the same provisions as other DOD infrastructure projects. Finally, DOD should take immediate action to ensure that its funding of living arrangements for the benefit of people with disabilities comports with federal disability-rights policy. To this end, DOD should move to adopt a specific policy that recognizes the need to end institutional bias and related forms of isolation and exclusion and create meaningful and affordable opportunities to receive community-based long-term services.

PART 9. RECOMMENDATIONS AND FUTURE DIRECTIONS

The foregoing parts have analyzed the application of U.S. federal disability law and policy in foreign assistance. Research has explored the implications of the adoption of the UN Convention on the Rights of Persons with Disabilities, especially in the context of overseas foreign assistance. The review examined the application of disability inclusion in the following realms of U.S. foreign assistance programming: (1) employment opportunities for people with disabilities; (2) access and inclusion of people with disabilities in U.S.-funded development programs; and (3) accessibility for people with disabilities to U.S.-funded construction and infrastructure projects. This part sets forth concrete recommendations flowing from the study and charts a strategy for the future. If followed, strategic implementation will position the United States to maintain a leadership role in disability inclusion in U.S. Government-funded overseas programs, facilities, and employment opportunities.

NCD Recommendations Directed to Congress

- **Apply Federal Disability Standards to Overseas Programs and Employment**
  NCD recommends that Congress instruct USAID, DOS, DOD, and other U.S. Government agencies operating overseas that Sections 501, 503, and 504 of the Rehabilitation Act of 1973 apply to overseas programs and employment opportunities operated by the U.S. Government. This will ensure that Americans with disabilities working for the U.S. Government are afforded the same protections abroad as in the United States. It will also foster disability inclusion in U.S.-funded overseas development programs.

- **Ensure Respect for Domestic Disability Laws in the Implementation of Overseas Programs in Host Countries**
  NCD recommends that Congress instruct USAID, DOS, DOD, and other U.S. Government agencies operating overseas to promote greater comparative knowledge and understanding of local disability law and policy frameworks, including the status of CRPD ratification in countries receiving foreign assistance. Enhancing understanding of local disability law and policy frameworks can foster opportunities for Rule of Law assistance and, importantly, foster compliance with host-country requirements, particularly in countries that have ratified the CRPD.

- **Limit Accessibility Waivers and Exceptions in Infrastructure to Avoid Future Redevelopment Costs**
  NCD recommends that the waivers and exceptions currently outlined in the Architectural Barriers Act of 1968 and regulations for building temporary structures in time of emergency be narrowed. The current exceptions are overly broad and create a gaping loophole for U.S.

Government agencies and their contractors. Qualifications for exceptions must be narrowed in order to promote accessible construction and to avoid future redevelopment costs in barrier removal. In addition, further clarity must be given to defining "emergency" and "temporary" pursuant to these exceptions.

- **Ratify the Convention on the Rights of Persons with Disabilities** NCD recommends that the Senate, upon receipt of the ratification package, consider and expeditiously provide its advice and consent to ratification of the CRPD.

NCD Recommendations Directed to USAID, DOS, and DOD

- **Promote Employment of People with Disabilities in Overseas Offices and Programs** USAID, DOS, and DOD should promote employment opportunities for people with disabilities in missions, embassies, consular offices, and overseas programs. Americans with disabilities have the right to equal access to employment opportunities and are entitled to reasonable accommodations to perform their job duties. This should include the opportunity to work in U.S. embassies, missions, and U.S. Government-funded programs abroad. It is therefore important for U.S. Government agencies to ensure that Americans with disabilities are afforded the same protections and remedies overseas as in the United States. Further, where local nationals are utilized, local nationals with disabilities should be hired to work in U.S.-funded overseas programs and facilities.

NCD Recommendations Directed to USAID
- **Revise the USAID Disability Policy** NCD recommends that USAID review and update its 2004 Disability Policy. The current policy, drafted in 1997, is outdated and provides little to no guidance as to *how* USAID programs can be made inclusive across all sectors of its development portfolio. The emergence of disability-inclusive policies by numerous bilateral and multilateral donors, spurred by the adoption of the CRPD, makes such a review timely; it also offers an opportunity for USAID to emerge, once again, as a preeminent leader in disability-inclusive development. The Disability Coordinator at USAID, placed within the

newly (re)established Bureau of Policy, Planning and Learning, is well positioned to undertake such a review.

- **Provide Adequate Resources for the Coordinator on Disability and Inclusive Development**

  NCD recommends that USAID provide ample resources for the Coordinator on Disability and Inclusive Development to advance implementation of the USAID Disability Policy. USAID should provide proper staffing and finances for this work and should promote agency-wide coordination. Additionally, USAID should promote interagency coordination between this office and DOS to promote disability inclusion in all international diplomacy and development work.

- **Introduce Mandatory Training in Disability Rights and Disability Inclusion in Development**

  NCD recommends that USAID, DOS, and DOD implement mandatory disability rights and disability inclusion in development training sessions for employees at all missions and embassies. The findings of this report indicate that personnel around the world are unfamiliar with strategies for disability inclusion in facilities, programs, and employment opportunities. Ensuring the participation of people with disabilities, DPOs, and inclusive-development experts should be a core component of any training strategy. Currently, USAID encourages employees to take the e-learning course. Introducing mandatory training would enhance participation across USAID. In addition, disability training should relate directly to inclusion strategies across specific sectors of development (e.g., economic development, democracy and governance, humanitarian assistance, public health, education) and connect to the specific responsibilities of various personnel (e.g., cognizant technical officers, budget officers). The development of any e-training course materials should be reviewed by inclusive-development experts and periodically updated to incorporate emerging best practices.

- **Require Disability-Inclusive Guidance in Statements of Work**

  NCD recommends that USAID issue a policy directive for RFAs and RFPs that requires meaningful disability inclusion in solicitation statements of work. The current practice under AAPD 04-17—burying the Disability Policy in the "Special Contract Requirements" section—is unlikely to draw more than the superficial attention of applicants and offerors. Crafting statements of work to more meaningfully include a disability dimension—for example, including people with disabilities as program beneficiaries or requiring a detailed plan for inclusion in relevant programs—is far more likely to yield offeror responses. There is a ready model for this type of approach in gender statements in statements of work.[383]

- **Incorporate Disability Inclusion in Technical Evaluation Criteria in USAID Solicitations**
  NCD recommends that, in order to foster meaningful disability inclusion in program design at the proposal stage, technical evaluation criteria must specify disability inclusion and must include a point allocation. Such an approach will compel applicants and offerors to emphasize their technical approach to disability inclusion and implementation of the disability policy. Disability inclusion in the technical evaluation criteria currently serve as the standard against which technical approaches are evaluated and indicate to applicants and offerors issues of significance for USAID. This could be accomplished in various ways, for example, through a disability-specific criterion of inclusion or as a component of the technical approach criteria. Consideration could also be given to the formulation of disability-specific criteria under the monitoring and evaluation criteria, for instance, by specifying disaggregation on the basis of disability in criteria concerning the clear definition of targets and relevant target populations.

- **Develop Disability Indicators and Strengthen Monitoring of Inclusion**
  NCD recommends that USAID require applicants and offerors to develop and outline disability indicators for use in performance monitoring plans. Given the commitment to strengthening USAID's monitoring and evaluation, as underscored in the QDDR, such an approach seems timely and readily achievable.

- **Provide Specifications for Costing Reasonable Accommodations**
  NCD recommends that USAID provide specific instructions for applicants and offerors in the preparation of the cost proposal in all USAID solicitations for costing of reasonable accommodations and modifications for people with disabilities. A line item in the cost proposal for proper costing of reasonable accommodations should be specified in these instructions and in accompanying charts.

- **Strengthen the Capacity of DPOs**
  NCD recommends that USAID fund capacity building for DPOs as a part of its civil society strengthening program within the Democracy and Governance Sector. Consistent with USAID's work to mobilize constituencies for reform through CSO development, USAID should redouble its efforts to provide funding to DPOs to build their capacity to undertake disability law and policy reform, collaborate with partner organizations, manage funds, research funding opportunities, and draft proposals, among other skills that are essential to sustain inclusive development programs. Such results can be achieved through programming that targets DPO capacity building and as a component of larger-scale CSO capacity building.

NCD Recommendations Directed to DOS

- **Issue Policy Statement on Rehabilitation Act Compliance**
  NCD recommends that DOS issue an official policy statement on compliance requirements for Sections 501, 503, and 504 of the Rehabilitation Act. DOS must make it clear to all federal employees that Sections 501, 503, and 504 apply to all U.S. programs, facilities, and employment opportunities overseas.
- **Provide Adequate Resources for the Office of the Special Advisor on International Disability Rights**
  NCD recommends that DOS provide ample resources for the Special Advisor on International Disability Rights to effectively promote disability inclusion across all DOS work. To this end, DOS should provide proper staffing and finances for this office and should promote agency-wide coordination. The office is situated in the DRL bureau and DOS should advance the work of this office across all DOS bureaus. Additionally, DOS should promote interagency coordination between this office and USAID to promote disability inclusion in all international diplomacy and development work.
- **Improve Embassy Accessibility**
  NCD recommends that all embassies, consular offices, and missions be made accessible to people with disabilities. Entranceways, meeting rooms, bathrooms, and other areas must be accessible. Further, information and materials must be accessible and available to people with disabilities. This includes visa applications, websites, and informational pamphlets and brochures, among other materials distributed to the public by embassies, consular offices, and missions.

Embassies, consular offices, and missions should provide sign
language interpreters, readers, or other services as requested by people
with disabilities who visit these facilities.

- **Deepen Disability Rights Coverage in Country Human Rights Reports**
  NCD recommends that DOS strengthen its disability rights coverage
  in its Human Rights Reports. Human Rights Officers should be
  encouraged to consult with local DPOs when drafting Country
  Reports within its Human Rights Reports. Facilitating the
  participation of DPOs in information gathering for the Country
  Reports on human rights will add depth and breadth to the content of
  the reports and help ensure coverage of the human rights situation of
  people with disabilities.

- **Enhance Access to Information on Cultural Exchange Programs**
  NCD recommends that DOS support trainings for staff of cultural
  exchange programs on the inclusion of people with disabilities and
  consider adopting specific disability inclusive mission statements or
  policies that encourage qualified people with disabilities to apply.
  NCD further recommends that DOS undertake measures to ensure that
  all information on programs is in accessible alternative formats
  (website materials, print, and in person) and that accessible housing
  options are available for participants with disabilities, along with
  individualized accommodations.

NCD Recommendations Directed to DOD

- **Limit Accessibility Waivers and Exceptions in Infrastructure to Avoid Future Redevelopment Costs**
  NCD recommends that DOD limit the number of waivers and
  exceptions permitted under its newly adopted ABA *Accessibility
  Standards for DOD Facilities*. Waivers and exceptions have been
  used throughout the world to build inaccessible infrastructure that
  later must be retrofitted to provide accessibility at a very high cost to
  American taxpayers. DOD should closely review waivers and
  exceptions prior to authorizing them to ensure they are used only in
  narrowly defined circumstances and only where necessary.

- **Provide Clear Accessibility Guidelines for New Infrastructure in Developing Countries**
  NCD recommends that DOD provide clear guidance to contractors on
  the application of the ABA Accessibility Standards in developing

countries. At present, the standards state they apply "worldwide," but there is a gap in the standards that allows for contractors to apply for waivers or argue for an exception in developing countries. These standards must clearly indicate that DOD infrastructure projects in developing countries are subject to the same provisions as other DOD infrastructure projects.

ANNEX I. COUNTRY LIST

Sub-Saharan Africa:

Ghana
Mozambique
Namibia
Sierra Leone
Uganda
Zambia

Europe and Eurasia:

Armenia
Russia
Serbia
Ukraine

Asia:

Bangladesh
India
Indonesia
Nepal
Philippines
Vietnam

Middle East:

Egypt

Latin America and the Caribbean:

Colombia
Ecuador
Mexico

ANNEX 2. QUESTION SET ON EMBASSY ACCESSIBILITY

NOTE: Two "desk-based" research questions before setting out to interview on site:

a. Is there a TTY number listed on the embassy's website?
b. Is the embassy's website accessible to screen-readers?

Accessibility of Embassy:

A. Is the embassy physically accessible?

1. Can a person come into the U.S. embassy building at street level or are there stairs at the entry of the building?

1a. If there are stairs, is there a ramp leading into the building?

1. No
2. Yes

If yes, please look at the ramp and evaluate how accessible the ramp is. (Note: We are looking for general comments about the slope of the ramp, how easily accessible it is to the main or other entrance of the building, how easy it is to get to and from the street: i.e.: very steep slope descending into busy street; gentle slope from sidewalk to main entryway; moderate slope into back entryway).

1b. Please describe any alternatives in place to allow access to the building for those with mobility impairments (i.e.: neither street/floor-level entry, nor ramp, but lift available, etc.):

2. Once in the building, if the building is more than one story, is there an elevator that is wheelchair accessible?

3. If there is an elevator, does the elevator work?

4. Is the entire building accessible to people who use wheelchairs? If no, what sections are unavailable?

5. Are there accessible bathrooms?

6. Are doorways wide enough for a wheelchair user to pass through?

7. If the entire building is not accessible to people with mobility impairments, does the embassy have a policy of holding meetings in areas of the building that are accessible? Please describe:

B. Is the embassy accessible to people who are deaf or hard of hearing?

8. Is a sign language interpreter available upon request?

9. If a sign language interpreter is available, whom do you have to go to in order to arrange for the sign language interpreter to come?

10. If a sign language interpreter is available, how soon can the interpreter arrive at the embassy once called?

11. If a sign language interpreter is available, are funds available to pay for this person's time?

12. Have you ever seen an interpreter at the embassy? (If yes, describe.)

13. Has the embassy employee ever called an interpreter in for any meeting he or she has run?

C. Is the embassy accessible to people who are blind or visually impaired?

14. Are informational materials and forms available in large print?

15. Are informational materials and forms available in Braille?

16. If information is available in either large print or Braille, how much and what types of information (i.e.: most/some/selected materials)? And if so, what materials are selected to be in large print or Braille?

17. Whom do you go to if you need something put in large print or Braille and how do you get this funded?

18. Does the embassy provide a reader upon request?

Part II: Programs in Embassies

19. Is there someone in this embassy who is the focal point for disability issues?

20. Has embassy staff ever received guidance/training on disability issues as part of their mission in working with the public or with the local government? If so, please describe the training:

21. How often do you see persons with disabilities coming to the embassy for programs, information, or meetings (that is, often/infrequently/never)? Please explain:

22. Can you describe any adjustments in programs or resource availability designed to ensure accessibility by persons with disabilities to events or programs run by the embassy?

23. Please describe any contact you or other members of the embassy staff have/had with local Disabled Peoples Organizations (DPOs) or NGOs that provide services to persons with disabilities?

24. Is any member of your staff—either U.S. embassy staff or local staff— disabled? (We do not need names; we just want to know if people with disabilities work there.)

25. To your knowledge, does the embassy have an explicit policy on employing people with disabilities from within the country?

26. To your knowledge, does the embassy encourage participation by people with disabilities in programs at the embassy that are not specifically disability-related?

27. Are there any laws or rules that guide you or that you must follow regarding persons with disabilities at your embassy?

28. Are you familiar with the Convention on the Rights of Persons with Disabilities and if so, can you tell me about this?

29. Do you here at the embassy receive directives, information, resources, or other communications or trainings on persons with disabilities through the State Department in Washington, USAID, or other U.S. agencies? If yes, could you describe these?

30. Are there any additional issues regarding accessibility and work or programs going on in the embassy related to persons with disabilities that I should be asking you about or anything else you would like to add related to this topic that I have not brought up?

31. Follow-up question: If this is the first time you have thought about either accessibility of your embassy building or accessibility of embassy programs for persons with disabilities, is there anything you would recommend be done to improve accessibility?

ANNEX 3. QUESTION SET ON USAID PROGRAMS ANDPOLICIES

Part I. Inclusion of People with Disabilities in Current Programming

1. Please describe how USAID programs in-country include people with disabilities routinely as members of the general populations reached by USAID programs:

1a) Please describe the efforts made to track the numbers of persons with disabilities reached or monitor or evaluate their opinion of your programs within the larger programs you offer:

2. Please describe any accommodations or modifications to programming made for people with disabilities to enable them to be included in non-disabilityspecific USAID projects or programs in this country:

3. Please describe any USAID programs geared specifically toward people with disabilities:

4. If these programs exist, how many people with disabilities do you think these USAID programs reach or impact?

5. What areas in the Democracy and Governance sector does your mission work on (for example, Rule of law, elections and political party building, civil society, governance, etc.)?

Note: Please only ask Questions 6, 7, and 8 if the persons indicated the mission runs that type of program. For example, if they tell you they do Rule-of-law work, then only ask them Question 6.

6. In the Rule-of-law sector, what training is provided on the legal rights of people with disabilities?

6a) Further, what programs or activities were developed in relation to the legal rights of people with disabilities?

7. In the Elections sector, what programs have you developed to increase people with disabilities' ability to participate in elections?

7a) Describe any specific accommodations made for people with disabilities to access electoral systems:

8. In the civil-society sector, how have you involved disabled people's organizations in civil-society or capacity-building programs?

9. Please describe any programs in which the USAID mission contributed with disabilities:

10. Please discuss whether the USAID mission in which you work sought funding for disability programs under the Disability Fund or other specific funds:

11. Please describe any contacts USAID has with local organizations that advocate for the rights of people with disabilities, or provide services or program support for people with disabilities:

12. If you are in contact with local organizations that advocate for people with disabilities, or provide services for people with disabilities, are these organizations run by people with disabilities themselves (disabled people's organizations, or DPOs)?

Or are they services run for people with disabilities?

13. Please describe any USAID programs run at "group homes," or USAIDfunded work dealing with "group homes" in any way:

Also, please describe any funding or programs that this mission has provided for local orphanages:

14. Please describe the mission's recruitment procedure for people with disabilities from within the country:

15. What accommodations (or modifications to programs) are in place to ensure inclusion of people with disabilities in USAID programs?

16. Please describe any training you have received at USAID on disability issues:

17. Please describe where the focal point at USAID is at the country level for questions about people with disabilities or disability issues:

18. Please describe any resources, places to get information, or guidance on disability issues within USAID at the regional level or from Washington:

19. Please explain any other places you go/would go to find out about disability in development issues:

20. Please describe any discussions you have had about disability issues/inclusion of people with disabilities with your colleagues here in country:

21. Please describe any USAID policies that pertain to people with disabilities:

22. Please describe U.S. laws that pertain to people with disabilities:
After they have answered, ask about the Americans with Disabilities Act if they do not bring it up or if they ask what relevance it has to the in-country work they are doing now:

23. Please describe international laws/laws in-country regarding people with disabilities:
After they have answered, ask if they have heard anything about the Convention on the Rights of Persons with Disabilities. If they have heard of it, ask them to tell you more about it:

24. Is there anything else regarding in-country work and people with disabilities that I should be asking you about or that you think is important for me to know?

25) Follow-up question: If this is the first time you have thought about inclusion of people with disabilities in in-country work, is there anything you would recommend be done to ensure inclusion of people with disabilities in future programs? (What do you suggest would be beneficial?)

In 1995, NCD was designated by the Department of State to be the U.S. Government's official contact point for disability issues.

End Notes

[1] World Health Organization [hereafter WHO] and the World Bank [hereafter WB], *Summary: World Report on Disability*, 7–8 (2011).

[2] *Id.* at 7.

[3] WHO and WB, *supra* note 1, at 8.

[4] *See* Leandro Despouy, *Human Rights and Disabled Persons* (Study Series 6), Centre for Human Rights, Geneva, and United Nations, New York (1993).

[5] *See* S. Peters, "Education for All: Including Children with Disabilities," *Education Notes* (August 2003). *See also* D. Filmer, "Disability, Poverty and Schooling in Developing Countries: Results from 14 Household Surveys," 22 *WB Econ. Rev.* 141–63 (2008).

[6] UN Secretary-General, UN, *Social Development: Questions Relating to the World Social Situation and to Youth, Aging, Disabled Persons and the Family, Implementation of the World Programme of Action Concerning Disabled Persons and the United Nations Decade of Disabled Persons*, paragraph 5, address before the General Assembly (September 11, 1992), UN Document A/CONF.47/415.

[7] *See* Jen Betts and Jonathan Flower, "Towards a Level Playing Field: A Call to Make Development Programs More Inclusive," in *All Things Being Equal 7* (World Vision, Autumn 2001). *See also* Jonathan Flower, *Mid-term Evaluation of CBR Programme in Mandalay and Rangoon*, report written for World Vision and DFID, UK, 2001.

[8] Human rights violations against people with disabilities, many of an egregious nature, are persistent, ongoing, and take many forms. *See, for example*, Disability Rights International [hereafter DRI] (formerly Mental Disability Rights International), *Human Rights and Mental Health: Mexico*, 13–41 (2000); DRI, *Children in Russia's Institutions: Human Rights and Opportunities for Reform*, 10–23 (1999); Mental Disability Advocacy Center [hereafter MDAC], *Cage Beds: Inhuman and Degrading Treatment or Punishment in Four EU Accession Countries*, 36–41 (2003), http://mdac.info/sites/mdac.info/ files/English Cage%20Beds.pdf; DRI, *Behind Closed Doors: Human Rights Abuses in the Psychiatric Facilities, Orphanages and Rehabilitation Centers of Turkey*, 24–25 (2005), http://www.mdri.org/PDFs/reports/turkey%20final%209-26-05.pdf; DRI, *Torture Not Treatment: Electric Shock and Long-Term Restraint in the United States on Children and Adults with Disabilities at the Judge Rotenberg Center*, 1–3, 12–13 (2010), http://www.mdri.org/PDFs/USReportandUrgentAppeal.pdf; Human Rights Watch, *As If We Weren't Human* (August 26, 2010), http://www.hrw.org/en/reports/ 2010/08/26/if-we-weren-t-human; DRI, *Abandoned and Disappeared: Mexico's Segregation and Abuse of Children and Adults with Disabilities* (2010), http://www.disabilityrightsintl.org/media-gallery/our-reports-publications/.

[9] Convention on the Rights of Persons with Disabilities [hereafter CRPD], GA Res 61/106, UN Doc A/RES/61/106 (December 13, 2006).

[10] *See* Janet E. Lord et al., World Bank, *Disability and International Cooperation and Development: A Review of Policies and Practices* (Social Protection Discussion Paper No. 1003, May 2010), http://siteresources.worldbank.org/DISABILITY/Resources/Publi cations-Reports/Disability and Intl Cooperation.pdf; *see also* Michael Ashley Stein,

Charlotte McClain-Nhlapo, and Janet E. Lord, *Disability Rights, the MDGs and Inclusive Development in Millennium Development Goals and Human Rights: Past, Present and Future* (Malcolm Langford et al., eds., 2011).

[11] *See* U.S. Agency for International Development [hereafter USAID], "Disability Initiatives," http://www.usaid.gov/about usaid/disability/.

[12] *Id.*

[13] *Development aid rose in 2009 and most donors will meet 2010 aid targets,* Organisation for Economic Co-operation and Development [hereafter OECD], April 14, 2010, http://www.oecd.org/document/11/0,3343,en 2649 34447 44981579 1 1 1 374 13,00.html; OECD iLibrary, *Development aid: Net official development assistance (ODA),* http://www.oecd-ilibrary.org/development/development-aid-net-official-development-assistance-oda20743866-table1.

[14] U.S. Department of State [hereafter DOS] and USAID, *Quadrennial Diplomacy and Development Review: Leading through Civilian Power* [hereafter QDDR] (December 2010), http://www.usaid.gov/qddr/QDDRFullReportHi.pdf.

[15] Department of Defense [hereafter DOD], *Quadrennial Defense Review Report* [hereafter *QDR*] (February 2010), http://www.defense.gov/qdr/qdr%20as%20of %2029jan10%201600.PDF.

[16] DOS and USAID, *supra* note 14.

[17] Annex 1 lists the selected countries. Of the 20 selected countries, in-country interviews and assessments were undertaken in 14. Desk-based research and focus group conference calls were conducted for the remaining six.

[18] Note that it was difficult in some cases to set up interviews in-country. This in itself may be a reflection of the low priority given to disability issues and the fact that many staff felt a lack of expertise in this area. For example, the local advocate in Serbia noted:

The USAID contacts were identified quite quickly with the assistance/engagement of our initial contact, executive officer. USAID staff seemed very willing to cooperate and they even facilitated meetings with their partner civil society organizations. There were some problems with availability of the director of democracy and government program, but we managed to get an interview with him even though it took more than one month to schedule a meeting (because of his frequent travels outside of the country). Both identifying and arranging interviews with the U.S. embassy officials was far more complicated. The highest ranked officials were highly nonresponsive. It took us several email inquiries to deputy chief of mission to learn that she was leaving the mission at the time, but in three weeks of trying to establish correspondence with her (while copying her colleague who referred us to her in the first place) we never received this information.

-Lea Simokovic, Program Associate, Serbia Office, DRI.

[19] For the question set, see Annex 2. Note that only basic accessibility issues were examined. While the Americans with Disabilities Act Accessibility Guidelines (ADAAG) were considered in developing the question set, the full checklist was not used.

[20] The extensive desk-based research included (1) programmatic review of USAID mission facilities and U.S. embassy websites for the 20 selected countries; (2) review of various DOD websites, with a particular emphasis on construction of infrastructure; (3) review of reports provided by USAID, DOS, and DOD personnel; and (4) review of USAID solicitations to determine compliance with the USAID Disability Policy and directives.

[21] Americans with Disabilities Act of 1990 [hereafter ADA], 42 U.S.C. §§ 12101-12213 (2000).

[22] Rehabilitation Act of 1973, Pub. L. No. 93-112, 87 Stat. 355 (1973).

[23] *Id.*

[24] Section 501 of the Rehabilitation Act establishes a federal Interagency Committee on Employees Who Are Individuals with Disabilities. 29 U.S.C. § 791(a) (1991). Section 503 of the Rehabilitation Act requires every contract or subcontract of $10,000 or more with any federal department or agency to "contain a provision requiring that the party contracting with the United States shall take affirmative action to employ and advance in employment qualified individuals with disabilities." 29 U.S.C. § 793. 29 U.S.C. § 794 applies to recipients of federal financial assistance.

[25] ADA, Pub. L. No. 101-336, 104 Stat. 327 (1990).

[26] 42 U.S.C. § 12101(a)(2) (1990).

[27] ADA, Pub. L. No. 101-336, § 201(c), 104 Stat. 327 (1990).

[28] Title I pertains to employment; Title II to public entities; Titles III to public accommodations; Title IV to telecommunications; and Title V to other miscellaneous provisions. ADA, Pub. L. No. 101-336, tit. I-V, 104 Stat. 327 (1990).

[29] 42 U.S.C § 12111(9) (2000); 42 U.S.C. § 12182 (b)(2) (2000).

[30] 20 U.S.C.A. §§ 1400 et seq. Under IDEA, public schools are required to provide all children with disabilities a "free appropriate public education in the least restrictive environment appropriate to their individual needs." *Id.*

[31] Fair Housing Amendments Act of 1988, Pub. L. No. 100-430, 102 Stat. 1619 (codified at 42 U.S.C. §§ 3601-3619, 3631 (1988), and 28 U.S.C. §§ 2341-2342 (1988). Prohibits discrimination against people with disabilities in housing.

[32] Architectural Barriers Act of 1968, 42 U.S.C. §§ 4151-4157 (1968).

[33] Air Carrier Access Act, 49 U.S.C. § 41795 (1986).

[34] Telecommunications Act of 1996, 47 U.S.C. §§ 153, 255 (1996).

[35] U.S. Const. art. I, § 8, cl. 3. The U.S. Constitution gives Congress broad powers "to regulate Commerce with foreign Nations." See *EEOC v. Arabian Am. Oil Co.*, 499 U.S. at 248 (1991) [hereafter *Aramco*]. Citing *Foley Bros. v. Filardo*, 336 U.S. 281, 284-285 (1949). *See also, Hartford Fire Ins. v. Cal.*, 509 U.S. 764 (1949); *Ford v. U.S.*, 273 U.S. 593 (1927); *American Banana Co. v. United Fruit Co.* 213 U.S. 341, 356 (1909) [hereafter *United Fruit*].

[36] The first known case was *Murray v. The Charming Betsy*, 6 U.S. (2 Cranch.) 64, at 118 (1804), where the Court stated, "[A]n Act of Congress ought never to be construed to violate the law of nations, if any possible construction remains." A century later, Justice Oliver Wendell Holmes stated, "The general and almost universal rule is that the character of an act as lawful or unlawful must be determined wholly by the law of the country where the act is done," *United Fruit* at 357.

[37] *See, for example*, Sisal, 274 U.S.268 at 276 (1927); *Alcoa*, 148 F.2d at 416 (1945); for examples of extraterritorial criminal cases, see *U.S. v. Bowman*, 260 U.S. 94 (1922); U.S. v. Plummer, 221 F.3d 1298 (11th Cir. 2000); U.S. v. Harvey, 2 F.3d 1318 (3d Cir. 1993); United States v. Larsen, 952 F.2d 1099 (9th Cir. 1991).

[38] Legislative history includes the recorded statements of Congress during the passage of a particular law.

[39] *Spector v. Norwegian Cruise Line Ltd.*, *545 U.S. 119 (2005)*.

[40] *Aramco*, 499 U.S., at 248.

[41] *Id.*

[42] *Id.*

[43] *Id.*

[44] *Id.*

[45] Justice Thurgood Marshall wrote for the dissent joined by Justice Harry Blackmun and Justice John Paul Stevens, arguing that the question of whether Title VII protects U.S. citizens from discrimination by U.S. employers abroad turns solely on congressional intent. "Contrary to the majority's analysis, this canon is not 'clear statement' rule of which relieves a court of the duty to give effect to all indicia of the legislative will.... when these tools are brought to bear on the issue in this case, the conclusion is inescapable that Congress did intend Title VII to protect United States citizens from discrimination by United States employers operating overseas." *Id.* at 261.

[46] The Court stated, "We assume that Congress legislates against the backdrop of the presumption against extraterritoriality. Therefore, unless there is 'the affirmative intention of the Congress clearly expressed,' ...we must presume it 'is primarily concerned with domestic conditions.'" *Id.* at 258 (citations omitted).

[47] Following the Court's decision in *Aramco*, Rep. William Jefferson (D-LA) introduced H.R. 1694, American Employees Equity Act of 1991, Rep. Kweisi Mfume (D-MD) introduced H.R. 1741, Extraterritorial Employment Protection Amendments of 1991, and Sen. John Danforth (R-MO) introduced S.1407, Protection of Extraterritorial Employment, together with Sen. Edward Kennedy's (D-MA) bills comprising the Civil Rights Act.

[48] Congress amended the Civil Rights Act of 1991 to give extraterritorial protection to American citizens working overseas for American employers. Civil Rights Act Amendments Act of 1991, Pub. L. No. 102-166, § 109, 105 Stat. 1071 (1991) (codified as amended at 42 U.S.C. § 2000e-1 (1994)). Civil Rights Act Amendments Act of 1991 § 3(4). See 29 U.S.C. §§ 621-634 (1999). The 1984 extraterritorial amendments are at 29 U.S.C. §§ 623(f) (1), 623(h).

[49] See 42 U.S.C. § 12101(a)(4) (1990).

[50] National Council on Disability, *Foreign Policy and Disability: Legislative Strategies and Civil Rights Protections to Ensure Inclusion of People with Disabilities* [hereafter, *NCD, Foreign Policy and Disability*], at 45 (September 9, 2003), http://www.ncd.gov/publications /2003/Sept92003.

[51] *Spector, 545 U.S.*

[52] Title III of the ADA prohibits discrimination against people with disabilities in the full and equal enjoyment of public accommodations, 42 U.S.C. § 12182(a) (2000), and public transportation services, 42 U.S.C. § 12184(a) (2000).

[53] *Spector, 545 U.S.*, at 125.

[54] *Id.* at 120.

[55] 42 U.S.C. § 12101 (a), (b) (1990).

[56] ADA Amendments Act of 2008, Pub. L. No. 110-325 (2008). *See also Sutton v. United Air Lines, Inc.*, 527 U.S. 471 (1999), *Toyota Motor Mfg., KY, Inc. v. Williams*, 534 U.S. 184 (2002).

[57] 42 U.S.C. §§ 4151-4157 (1968).

[58] *Id.*

[59] *Id.*

[60] 42 U.S.C. § 12112 (1990).

[61] Civil Rights Act Amendments Act of 1991 § 109(a) (1990).

[62] *Id.*

[63] Curt Tarnoff and Larry Nowells, Congressional Research Service, OC 98-916, "Foreign Aid: An Introductory Overview of U.S. Programs and Policy," 30 (2004).

[64] *Id.*

[65] Rehabilitation Act of 1973, Pub. L No 93-112, 87 Stat. 355 (1973).

[66] Section 504 of the Rehabilitation Act of 1973, as amended 29 U.S.C. § 794 (1973).

[67] NCD, *Foreign Policy and Disability, supra* note 50, at 47. The report cites two federal cases where courts applied Section 504's protections to Americans abroad, reasoning that the individuals qualify for Section 504 protections when they are "in the United States." *Bird v. Lewis & Clark College*, 104 F. Supp. 2d 1271 (D. Or. 2000) aff'd 303 F.3d 1015 (9th Cir. 2002); *King v. Bd. of Control of E. Mich. Univ.*, 221 F. Supp.2d 783 (2002). One court found that Section 504 was applicable to a student who sought accommodations in a study-abroad program operated by an American college. *Bird*, 104 F. Supp. 2d. 1271 (2000). Further, in another case, a federal court noted that the phrase "qualified individual in the United States" applies to individuals who qualify for the law's protection in the United States, but does not limit the law's coverage to entities and programs located in the United States. There, the court held Section 504 applicable to "all federally funded programs, not only those in the United States." *King*, 221 F. Supp. 2d 783.

[68] Foreign Assistance Act, 22 U.S.C. § 2151 (1961).

[69] *Id.*

[70] Section 504 of the Rehabilitation Act of 1973, as amended 29 U.S.C. § 794 (1973); CRPD, *supra* note 9.

[71] Section 501 of the Rehabilitation Act of 1973, as amended 29 U.S.C. § 793 (1973).

[72] The EEOC is the federal administrative agency in the United States given judicial authority through the Administrative Procedures Act 5 U.S.C. §500 et seq. (APA) to interpret employment discrimination law. If a plaintiff or defendant wishes to appeal the EEOC's decision, he or she can appeal to a federal court. However, a higher level of deference is given to the EEOC's construction of a statute. "If the Court determines Congress has not directly addressed the precise question at issue, the court does not simply impose its own construction of the statute . . . rather...[i]f the statute is silent or ambiguous with respect to the specific question, the issue for the court is whether the agency's answer is based on a permissible construction of the statute." *Chevron U.S.A., Inc. v. National Resources Defense Council, Inc.*, 467 U.S. 837, 104 S. Ct. 2778, 81 L. Ed. 2d 694 (1984).

[73] *Katz v. Department of State*, EEOC No.0720060025 (2009).

[74] *Id.*

[75] *Id.*

[76] USAID, "Foreign Service Officer Frequently Asked Questions," http://www.usaid.gov/careers /fsofaq.html.

[77] *Katz*, EEOC No.0720060025.

[78] *Katz*, citing Lovell v. Department of Justice, EEOC Appeal No. 01A41642 (May 26, 2006).

[79] *Katz*, EEOC No.0720060025.

[80] *Id.*

[81] *Id.*

[82] Section 503 of the Rehabilitation Act of 1973, as amended 29 U.S.C. § 793 (1973).

[83] Section 503 of the Rehabilitation Act requires every contract or subcontract of $10,000 or more with any federal department or agency to "contain a provision requiring that the party contracting with the United States shall take affirmative action to employ and advance in employment qualified individuals with disabilities." 29 U.S.C. § 793. NCD, *Foreign Policy and Disability, supra* note 50.

[84] Section 508 of the Rehabilitation Act of 1973, as amended, 29 U.S.C. § 794d (a) (1) (A), http://www.access-board.gov/sec508/guide/act.htm; "Section 508 requirements are separate from, but complementary to, requirements in sections 501 and 504 of the Rehabilitation Act that require, among other things, that agencies provide reasonable accommodations for

employees with disabilities, provide program access to members of the public with disabilities, and take other actions necessary to prevent discrimination on the basis of disability in their programs." U.S. Census Bureau, *Section 508 Acquisition FAQs*, http://www.census.gov/procur/www/508-faq.html.

[85] Access Board, "Section 508 Homepage," http://www.access-board.gov/508.htm.

[86] Access Board, "The Rehabilitation Act Amendments (Section 508)," http://www.access-board.gov/sec508/guide/act.htm.

[87] CRPD, *supra* note 9, at art. 1.

[88] CRPD, *supra* note 9.

[89] For overviews of the CRPD and its reflection of the social model of disability, see Rosemary Kayess and Phillip French, "Out of darkness into light? Introducing the Convention on the Rights of Persons with Disabilities," 8 *Hum. Rts., L. Rev.*, 1–27 (2008); Janet E. Lord and Michael Ashley Stein, "The Domestic Incorporation of Human Rights Law and the United Nations Convention on the Rights of Persons with Disabilities," 83*Wash. L. Rev.*, 449, 452–56 (2008); Michael Ashley Stein and Janet E. Lord, "Future Prospects for the United Nations Convention on the Rights of Persons with Disabilities," in *The UN Convention on the Rights of Persons with Disabilities: European and Scandinavian Perspectives* 17 (Oddný Mjöll Arnardóttir and Gerard Quinn eds., 2009).

[90] Gerard Quinn, "Closing: Next Steps-Towards a United Nations Treaty on the Rights of Persons with Disabilities," *Disability Rights*, 519, 541 (Peter Blanck ed., 2005).

[91] For a discussion of the medical and charity models of disability, see Anna Lawson, "The United Nations Convention on the Rights of Persons with Disabilities: New Era or False Dawn?," 34 *Syracuse J. Int'l. L. & Com.*, 563 (2007). "[T]he medical or individual approach to disability has little to offer beyond a lifetime of unfulfilled potential and segregation. Unable to access mainstream education or employment, these people must depend for their survival on welfare benefits or charity." *Id.* at 571. *See also* Michael Ashley Stein and Penelope J. S. Stein, *Beyond Disability Civil Rights*, 58 *Hastings L. J.* 1203, 1206 (2007).

[92] *Id.*

[93] CRPD, *supra* note 9, at preambular para. (e).

[94] *Id.* at art. 2.

[95] *Id.* at art. 3.

[96] *Id.* at preambular para. (t).

[97] *Id.* at preambular para. (p).

[98] The White House Office of the Press Secretary, *Remarks by the President on Signing of U.N. Convention on the Rights of Persons with Disabilities Proclamation* (June 22, 2010), http://www.whitehouse.gov/the   press   office/Remarks-by-the-President-on-Rightsof-Persons-with-Disabilities-Proclamation-Signing/; United Nations, UN Enable Rights and Dignities of Persons with Disabilities, Convention and Optional Protocol Signatures and Ratifications, http://www.un.org/disabilities/countries.asp?navid=12&pid=166#U.

[99] Note that ratification is "the international act so named whereby a Sate establishes on the international plane its consent to be bound by a treaty." Vienna Convention, art. 2(1)(b). This should be distinguished from the approval of a treaty through domestic process (e.g., congressional or parliamentary). While "ratification" in the domestic legal context is quite often used to describe the domestic process of approval, this is different from ratification on the international plane. Anthony Aust, *Modern Treaty Law and Practice* (Cambridge University Press, 1st ed., 2000), 103 [hereafter Aust].

[100] §312(3) of the Restatement (Third) of the Foreign Relations Law of the United States is consistent with the Vienna Convention on the legal effects of signature and this is widely regarded as representing customary international law (1987). The Restatement provides, "Prior to the entry into force of an international agreement, a state that has signed the agreement, or expressed its consent to be bound is obliged to refrain from acts that would defeat the object and purpose of the agreement." *Id.* at 172. The obligation continues until the state has made clear its intention not to become a party to the treaty or where it appears that entry into force will be unduly delayed. *Id.* at Comment (i).

[101] The practice of the United States is consistent with the proposition that signature does carry some legal consequence. In 2002, under the George W. Bush Administration, the United States is said to have "unsigned" the International Criminal Court Statute. As Aust points out, this is not entirely correct from a legal standpoint, as signature is a physical act. Thus while signature as such cannot be undone, its legal effects can be effectively nullified. Aust, *supra* note 99 at 103.On May 6, 2002, the United States sent a diplomatic note to the depositary of the International Criminal Court (ICC), saying that it did not intend to become a party to the ICC. Press Release U.S. Department of State, International Criminal Court: Letter to UN Secretary General Kofi Annan (May 6, 2002), http://2001-2009.state.gov/r/pa/prs/ps/2002/9968.htm. In effect, therefore, its signature was withdrawn. While the United States has not ratified the Vienna Convention, its practice in this particular instance discloses evidence that it does accept most of the provisions. It is an uncontroversial proposition, therefore, that the Vienna Convention provision regarding signature is customary international law to which the United States is bound.

[102] Aust, *supra* note 99, at 119.

[103] U.S. Const. art. II, § 2, cl. 2.

[104] *Id.*

[105] *Id.*

[106] U.S. Const. art. VI, cl. 2.

[107] *See* NCD, *Finding the Gaps: A Comparative Analysis of Disability Laws in the United States to the United Nations Convention on the Rights of Persons with Disabilities* (Michael Ashley Stein and Michael Waterstone) (2008), http://www.ncd.gov/publications /2008/May122008.

[108] *See* CRPD, *supra* note 9, at art. 5.

[109] *Id.* at art. 2.

[110] *Id.*

[111] *See id.* at art. 9.

[112] *Id.*

[113] *Id.*

[114] *Id.*

[115] *Id.*

[116] *Id.*

[117] *Id.* at art. 4(1)(e).

[118] *See* Bill and Melinda Gates Foundation, *Global Development Program*, http://www.gatesfoundation.org/global-development/Pages/overview.aspx.

[119] CRPD, *supra* note 9, at art. 32(1).

[120] *Id.* at art. 32.

[121] *Id.* at art. 24.

[122] *Id.* at art. 27.

[123] *Id.* at art. 19.

[124] *Id.* at art. 9.

[125] *Id.* at art. 25.

[126] *Id.* at art. 13. The training of people in the justice system must have a disability component: "In order to help to ensure effective access to justice for persons with disabilities, States Parties shall promote appropriate training for those working in the field of administration of justice, including police and prison staff." *Id.* at art. 13(2).

[127] *See id.* at art. 8–30.

[128] The impact of these disasters on people with disabilities continues to serve as a major impetus for more inclusive disaster preparedness and response, both internationally as well as domestically in the United States. *See generally* Michael Stein and Michael Waterstone, "Disability Inclusive Development and Natural Disasters," in *Law and Recovery from Disaster: Hurricane Katrina*, 71 (Robin Paul Malloy, ed., 2008); International Disability Rights Monitor, *Disability and Tsunami Relief Efforts in India, Indonesia and Thailand* (2005), http://www.ideanet.org/cir/uploads/File/TsunamiReport.pdf. The appointment by President Obama of a senior disability advisor within the Federal Emergency Management Administration in the Department of Homeland Security is a salient domestic example of these developments.

[129] CRPD, *supra* note 9, at art. 11.

[130] *Id.* at art. 28, 28(2)(a), 28(2)(d).

[131] *Id.* at art. 25.

[132] *Id.* at art. 26.

[133] *Id.* at art. 20.

[134] *Id.* at art. 16.

[135] For more on USAID's democracy and governance programming, see "Overview," http://www.usaid.gov/our work/democracy and governance/.

[136] *See* CRPD, *supra* note 9, at art. 12.

[137] *Id.*

[138] *Id.*

[139] The otherwise useful publication, *Managing Assistance in Support of Political and Electoral Processes*, illustrates well the invisibility of disability in technical publications in this and other democracy and governance contexts. Nowhere in the publication are people with disabilities recognized as a disadvantaged and politically disenfranchised group and nowhere is any specific guidance given on intervention that might enhance their inclusion in political and electoral processes. *See* USAID/Center for Democracy and Governance, *Managing Assistance in Support of Political and Electoral Processes* (January 2000), http://www.usaid.gov/our work/democracy and governance/ publications/pdfs/pnacf631. pdf.

[140] *See* CRPD, *supra* note 9, at art. 13.

[141] *Id.* at art. 29.

[142] *Id.*

[143] *Id.*

[144] *Id.*

[145] *See generally* USAID, *A Guide to DCHA/DG Activities* [hereafter *DG User's Guide*], http://www.usaid.gov/ourwork/democracy and governance/publications/pdfs/ DG Activities Feb09 508c.pdf.

[146] This due process imperative is reinforced through the inclusion of participation as a general principle within Article 3, as a general state obligation in Article 4, and in addition to its

inclusion as a specific substantive right in Article 29 on participation in political and public life. CRPD, *supra* note 9.

[147] *See id.* at art. 32.

[148] *Id.* at art. 33.

[149] *See id.* at preamble para.

[150] *Id.* at art. 27.

[151] *See generally* Hervé Bernard et al., Handicap International, *Good Practices for Economic Inclusion of People with Disabilities: Funding Mechanisms for Self-Employment* (August 2006), http://www.handicap-international.org/uploads/media/goodpractices-GB2coul.PDF; S. Dyer, *The Inclusion of Disabled People in Mainstream Micro Finance Programs*, Disability and MF (April 7–9, 2003); Joshua Goldstein, *A New Financial Access Frontier: People with Disabilities*, (Center for Financial Inclusion at ACCION international concept paper, June 2010); C. Lewis, *Microfinance from the point of view of women with disabilities: Lessons from Zambia and Zimbabwe*, Oxfam GB 12 Gender and Development (2004).

[152] *See* DOS, "Bureau of Educational and Cultural Affairs," http://exchanges.state.gov/.

[153] *See* CRPD, *supra* note 9, at art. 30(1)(c). For detailed consideration of Article 30, see Janet E. Lord and Michael Ashley Stein, "Social Rights and the Relational Value of the Rights to Participate in Sport, Recreation and Play," 27 *BU Int'l L. J.* 249 (2009).

[154] *See* Lord, *supra* note 10. *See also* Katherine Guernsey, Marco Nicoli, and Alberto Ninio, *Convention on the Rights of Persons with Disabilities: Its Implementation and Relevance for the World Bank* 3 (World Bank, June 2007); GTZ, *Disability and Development: A Contribution to Promoting the Interests of Persons with Disabilities in German Development Cooperation* 2 (2006); AUSAID, *Development for All: Towards a Disability-Inclusive Australian Aid Program 2009–2014* (2008), http://www.ausaid.gov.au/keyaid /pdf/FINAL%20AusAIDDevelopment%20for%20All.pdf; UK Department for International Development, *How To Note: Working on disability in country programmes* (2007), http://webarchive.nationalarchives.gov.uk/+/http://www.dfid.gov.uk/pubs/files /DisguideDFID.pdf.

[155] USAID, "Disability and development," http://www.usaid.gov/about usaid/disability/ ; *See also* USAID, "Disability in Australia's aid program," http://www.ausaid. gov.au/keyaid/disability.cfm ; the United Nations Development Programme and other UN agencies and programs are likewise reconsidering their mandates in light of the CRPD, and the application of the CRPD to UN programming is being facilitated and coordinated through the Inter-Agency Support Group. The group is charged with coordinating the work of the United Nations system in support of the promotion and implementation of the Convention, which includes the development of a draft strategy and plan of action to mainstream the CRPD throughout the work of the UN system. For a summary of the work of the Inter-Agency Support Group, see Report of the Secretary-General, "Status of the Convention on the Rights of Persons with Disabilities" (July 7, 2009), UN Doc. A/64/128, http://www.dcdd.nl/data/1252922023240 CRPD%2064.pdf (CRPD status).

[156] The origins of USAID may be traced to the Marshall Plan reconstruction of Europe after World War II and the Truman Administration's Point Four Program. In 1961, the Foreign Assistance Act was signed into law and USAID was created by executive order. *See* USAID, "About USAID," http://www.usaid.gov/about usaid/.

[157] The 2010 National Security Strategy articulates the objective of development as follows: "Through an aggressive and affirmative development agenda and commensurate resources, we can strengthen the regional partners we need to help us stop conflict and counter global

criminal networks; build a stable, inclusive global economy with new sources of prosperity; advance democracy and human rights; and ultimately position ourselves to better address key global challenges by growing the ranks of prosperous, capable and democratic states that can be our partners in the decades ahead."
The White House, National Security Strategy, (May 2010), http://www.whitehouse.gov /sites/default/files/rss viewer/national security strategy.pdf.

[158] *See* "About USAID," *supra* note 156. Note that while USAID is the lead agency for international development assistance, there are a number of other agencies that implement foreign assistance programming, including the U.S. Departments of State, Defense, Agriculture, Commerce, Justice, Labor, and Treasury, among others. The proliferation of the international programs of federal departments or agencies across the government presents a major challenge for disability inclusion, as it also does for the coherence and coordination of U.S. foreign assistance generally. For a useful critique of U.S. foreign policy and development policy, see Gerald F. Hyman, *Foreign Policy and Development: Structure, Process, Policy and the Drip-by-Drip Erosion of USAID*, The Center for Strategic and International Studies (September 27, 2010), http://csis.org/files/publication /100923 Hyman ForeignPolicyAndDevel Web.pdf.

[159] U.S. General Accounting Office, GAO/ NSIAD-91-82, "Foreign Assistance: Assistance to Disabled Persons in Developing Countries" (February 15, 1991), http://pdf.usaid.gov/pdf docs/PCAAA224.pdf.

[160] *Id.* at 2. For a review of efforts to ensure inclusion in foreign assistance programming, see NCD, *Foreign Policy and Disability, supra* note 50.

[161] NCD, *Foreign Policy and Disability* (1996), http://www.ncd.gov/publications/ 1996/08011996. There, NCD recommended (1) creating a comprehensive foreign policy on disability to advocate for people with disabilities through activities on international levels; (2) extending U.S. disability law by legislation or executive order to unambiguously include the international operations of the U.S. Government; (3) employing domestic standards of nondiscrimination in U.S.-sponsored international activities; (4) training U.S. foreign affairs agencies and their contractors to plan for programmatic accessibility; and (5) establishing the principle that no U.S. international activity should have a lower standard of inclusion than its domestic correlate.

[162] USAID, Policy Guidance, USAID Disability Policy Paper (September 12, 1997), http://pdf.usaid.gov/pdfdocs/PDABQ631.pdf.

[163] *Id.*

[164] Notably, the 1997 Policy Paper takes the position that "While the ADA applies to U.S. citizens (including USAID employees) overseas, it does not apply to non-U.S. citizens, who are the primary beneficiaries of USAID programs. The USAID Disability Policy is thus in part an effort to extend the spirit of the ADA in areas beyond the jurisdiction of U.S. law." *Id.* at 2.

[165] NCD, *Foreign Policy and Disability, supra* note 50.

[166] *See* USAID, "Disability Policy," http://www.usaid.gov/about usaid/disability/.

[167] *Id.*

[168] USAID, AAPD 04-17 USAID Acquisition and Assistance Disability Policy Directive, *Supporting USAID's Disability Policy in Contracts, Grants, and Cooperative Agreements* [hereafter AAPD 04-17] (December 17, 2004), http://www.usaid.gov/business/business opportunities/cib/pdf/aapd04 17.pdf; USAID, "AAPD 05-07 USAID Acquisition and Assistance Disability Policy Directive, *Supporting USAID's Standards for Accessibility for the Disabled in Contracts, Grants, and Cooperative Agreements* [hereafter AAPD 05-07]

(June 16, 2005), http://www.usaid.gov/business/business opportunities/cib/pdf/aapd05 07.pdf.

[169] According to the Directive, such information includes, among other things, advance notification of changes in acquisition or assistance regulations; reminders; procedures; and general information. Also, AAPDs may be used to implement new requirements on short notice, pending formal amendment of acquisition or assistance regulations. AAPD 04-17, *supra* note 174.

[170] *Id.*

[171] This language reads as follows:

"USAID Disability Policy - Acquisition (December 2004)

(a) The objectives of the USAID Disability Policy are (1) to enhance the attainment of United States foreign assistance program goals by promoting the participation and equalization of opportunities of individuals with disabilities in USAID policy, country and sector strategies, activity designs and implementation; (2) to increase awareness of issues of people with disabilities both within USAID programs and in host countries; (3) to engage other U.S. Government agencies, host country counterparts, governments, implementing organizations and other donors in fostering a climate of nondiscrimination against people with disabilities; and (4) to support international advocacy for people with disabilities. The full text of the policy paper can be found at the following website: http://pdf.usaid.gov/pdf docs/PDABQ631.pdf.

"(b) USAID therefore requires that the contractor not discriminate against people with disabilities in the implementation of USAID programs and that it make every effort to comply with the objectives of the USAID Disability Policy in performing this contract. To that end and within the scope of the contract, the contractor's actions must demonstrate a comprehensive and consistent approach for including men, women and children with disabilities." *Id.* at 2–3.

[172] Note that the required provision is substantially the same for RFPs and RFAs, but there are terminology differences between acquisitions and agreements that are applied in the required provisions.

[173] *See* USAID, *USAID Acquisition and Assistance Policy Directive (Disability Policy on New Construction)* (2005), http://www.usaid.gov/about usaid/disability/.

[174] *Id.*

[175] *Id.*

[176] *Id.* Note that the required provision is substantially the same for RFPs and RFAs, but there are terminology differences between acquisitions and agreements that are applied in the required provisions.

[177] In a review of 55 RFAs released between February and July 2010, 23 of the RFAs did not include the required disability provision. *See* USAID Brazil, Mozambique RFA512-10-000004, *Trilateral Cooperation—Food Security* (July 7, 2010); USAID RFA-111- 10-000004, *Support to Armenia-Turkey Rapprochement* (July 2, 2010). Further, the disability provision was included in only one of the 10 annual program statements (APSs) reviewed in the same time period.

[178] *See* USAID Southern Africa RFA 674-10-0051, *Support for Integrated Service Delivery* (July 7, 2010) (includes Disability Policy provision, but makes no mention of people with disabilities in any other section of the RFA).

[179] "The Agency recognizes that it does not have specific expertise in universal/accessible design. Therefore, the U.S. Access Board, an independent Federal agency devoted to accessibility for people with disabilities, is USAID's consultative partner in developing and maintaining

accessibility requirements and providing technical assistance and training on guidelines and standards. The Access Board and the list of resources included in this document provide additional technical information." USAID, *USAID Policy on Standards for Accessibility for the Disabled in USAID-Financed Construction*, http://pdf.usaid.gov/pdf docs/PDACG011. pdf.

[180] *Id.*

[181] AAPD 05-07, *supra* note 181.

[182] *Id.* at 1(f).

[183] *Id.* at 1(f)(2).

[184] USAID, ADS Series 300, 302: Acquisition and Assistance, 302.5.14 Supporting USAID's Disability Policy in Contracts, http://www.usaid.gov/policy/ads/300/302.pdf.

[185] *See supra* note 174.

[186] These reports are available on the USAID website at http://www.usaid.gov/about usaid/disability/pubs.html.

[187] USAID, *Fifth Report on the Implementation of USAID Disability Policy* [hereafter *Fifth Report*] (December 2008), http://pdf.usaid.gov/pdf docs/PDACM100.pdf.

[188] *Id.*

[189] *Id.* USAID, *Fourth Report on the Implementation of USAID Disability Policy* (November 2005), http://pdf.usaid.gov/pdf docs/PDACF599.pdf.

[190] *Fifth Report*, *supra* note 187.

[191] *d.*

[192] *Id.*

[193] *Id.*

[194] *Id.* Note that missions were not specifically asked to report on employment of people with disabilities. The missions that did report decided to include hiring in their self-reporting.

[195] *Id.*

[196] Consolidated Appropriations Act of 2005, § 579 (a), Pub. L. No. 106-447.

[197] *Id.*

[198] *Id.*

[199] "Disability Program Fund," USAID, http://www.usaid.gov/aboutusaid/disability.

[200] *Id.*

[201] USAID's Involvement in Promoting Disability Inclusion, March 8, 2011.

[202] *Id.*

[203] *Id.*

[204] *Id.*

[205] *Id.*

[206] "We found the understanding of disability issues and its inclusiveness in USAID programs is very low. They have one program focused on medical rehabilitation like providing different artificial and assistive devices to the persons with physical disabilities." Local advocate interview with USAID personnel, USAID, Nepal.

[207] Personnel from various missions indicated that they had never attended trainings on disability when they were offered. The officers interviewed in Armenia stated that the mission never offered any disability trainings, but they would like to attend such trainings if offered in the future. Further, there was a disability session at the democracy and governance officers training held in June 2010. Only a few people showed up at the session, as the majority of attendees elected to attend a session on "Legislative Web Portals" that was taking place at the same time.

[208] "Their partnership with DPOs for the strengthening and organizational development is almost nonexistent." USAID interview, Nepal, *supra* note 206.

[209] *Id. Final Write-Up after Interviews.*

[210] The officers interviewed in seven missions were not aware of the USAID Disability Policy.

[211] Local advocate interview with USAID personnel, USAID, Serbia.

[212] Local advocate interview with USAID personnel, USAID, Bangladesh.

[213] Review information on file.

[214] USAID West Bank/Gaza, RFA 294-2010-116, *Enhancing Palestine Independent Media* (Issued May 7, 2010).

[215] USAID Zambia, RFP 611 2011-02, *Institutional Support Program*; RFP 611 2011-04, *Improved Student Effectiveness Program.*

[216] Credible documentation of human rights abuses in congregate institutions, including orphanages, psychiatric hospitals, and other facilities, is now ubiquitous and was a major reason that the CRPD reflects the trend against such living arrangements in favor of community-based alternatives.

[217] USAID Caucasus, RFA 114-10-000001, *Social Infrastructure Project* (February 12, 2010).

[218] *Olmstead v. L.C.*, 527 U.S. 581 (1999).

[219] *See generally* DRI, *Not on the Agenda: Human Rights of People with Disabilities in Kosovo* (2002); *Human Rights & Mental Health: Mexico* (2000); *Children in Russia's Institutions: Human Rights and Opportunities for Reform* (1999); *Human Rights and Mental Health: Hungary* (1997); *Human Rights and Mental Health: Uruguay* (1995). These reports are available at http://www.MDRI.org. For a detailed report outlining specific abuses against people labeled with psychiatric disorders, see National Council on Disability, *From Privileges to Rights: People with Psychiatric Disabilities Speak Out for Themselves* (January 20, 2002) *available at* http://www.ncd.gov/publications/2000/Jan202000.

[220] DRI, *Hidden Suffering: Romania's Segregation and Abuse of Infants and Children with Disabilities*, http://www.disabilityrightsintl.org/wordpress/wp-content/uploads/ romania-May-9-final with-photos.pdf.

[221] DRI, *The Worldwide Campaign to End the Institutionalization of Children*, http://www. disabilityrightsintl.org/learn-about-the-worldwide-campaign-to-end-theinstitutionalization-of-children/.

[222] *Id.*

[223] USAID interview (1), Serbia, *supra* note 211.

[224] USAID interview, Nepal, *supra* note 206.

[225] *See* Lord and Stein, *supra* note 89.

[226] USAID interview, Bangladesh, *supra* note 212.

[227] *Id.*

[228] After meeting with USAID personnel in various missions, many local advocates reported that people with disabilities are not being included in all programs.

[229] Local advocate interviews at USAID in Serbia and Egypt revealed that only disability-specific programs provide accommodations or modifications for people with disabilities. USAID interview, Serbia, *supra* note 211; local advocate interview with USAID personnel, USAID, Egypt.

[230] USAID interview (2), Serbia, *supra* note 211. "We did not make such accommodations for the mere fact that there were no handicap people within the beneficiary group of our programs so far. For example, in programs dealing with Serbian media there were no journalists that were handicapped. Also, there wasn't anyone handicapped, or should I say disabled, in the

Ministry of Justice we worked with, at least to our knowledge. So, there was no need to make that type of accommodations or changes." *Id.*

[231] Local advocate interview with USAID personnel, USAID, Armenia.

[232] USAID, *USAID Evaluation Policy*, January 2011, http://www.usaid.gov/evaluation/ USAIDEvaluationPolicy.pdf "The evaluation policy sets out an ambitious recommitment to learn as we 'do,' updating our standards and practices to address contemporary needs. In an increasingly complex operating environment, the discipline of development demands a strong practice and use of evaluation as a crucial tool to inform our global development efforts, and to enable us to make hard choices based on the best available evidence." *Id.* at 5.

[233] "Strengthening Monitoring, Evaluation and Transparency," USAID Forward, http://forward. usaid.gov/reform-agenda/strengthening-monitoring-eval.

[234] *Id.* at 5.

[235] CRPD, *supra* note 9, at art. 31.

[236] Local advocate interview with USAID personnel, USAID, Vietnam.

[237] James W. Conroy, *Report of the Independent Evaluator on the Outcomes of the USAID Grant Entitled "Initiative for Inclusion: A Civil Society Support Program for Citizens with Mental Disabilities and Their Families in Kosovo* (July 2007) (citing DRI's original proposal to USAID).

[238] USAID Afghanistan, RFP 306-10-0034.

[239] QDDR, *supra* note 14, at 104.

[240] QDDR, *supra* note 14, at 76.

[241] *See* Lord, *supra* note 10.

[242] QDDR, *supra* note 14, at 90.

[243] *See* 2010 Presidential Policy Directive on Development (PPD).

[244] While the parameters of this review are limited, disability inclusion is highly relevant across all sectors of international development.

[245] USAID, "Disaster Assistance," http://www.usaid.gov/ourwork/ humanitarian assistance /disaster assistance/.

[246] *Id.*

[247] *Id.*

[248] *Id.*

[249] USAID, *General Information on Disability and Development* (2007), http://www.usaid.gov /ourwork/cross-cuttingprograms/wid/pubs/Disability InformationSept20071.pdf.

[250] *Id.*

[251] *Id.*

[252] USAID/OFDA, *Guidelines for Unsolicited Proposals and Reporting* (October 2008), http://www.usaid.gov/ourwork/humanitarianassistance/disasterassistance/resources/ pdf/updated guidelines unsolicited proposals reporting.pdf
These OFDA guidelines are intended to assist organizations in the preparation of proposals for new awards and award modifications and their submission to OFDA.

[253] The guidelines do note that "[b]eneficiaries can include those who had disabilities prior to, as well as resulting from, the disaster" and that "[d]isability activities can also include specific care, such as rehabilitation services or psychosocial support, for people with temporary or long-term disabilities caused by the disaster," yet this provides little in the way of information to foster meaningful implementation. *Id.*

[254] USAID, *Field Operations Guide (FOG) for Disaster Assessment and Response, Version 4.0* (September 2005), http://www.usaid.gov/our work/humanitarian assistance/disaster assistance/resources/pdf/fog v4.pdf.

[255] USAID, *Sample Detailed Budget for Primary Funding Recipients*, http://www.usaid.gov/our work/humanitarian assistance/disaster assistance/resources/.

[256] Private Voluntary Organization (PVO) InterAction Standards, revised January 6, 256 11, 7.4

[257] *Id.* at 7.4.1.

[258] The standards also call on members to consult with local partner organizations "in the field." *Id.* at 7.4.2

[259] *Id.* at 7.4.3

[260] *See* USAID, *Economic Growth and Trade*, http://www.usaid.gov/our work/ economic growth and trade/index.html.

[261] USAID, *Securing the Future: A Strategy for Economic Growth* 6 (2008), http://www.usaid.gov/our work/economic growth and trade/eg/eg strategy/ eg strategy v4 final.pdf.

[262] Note that other USAID strategies likewise are directed at promoting economic growth, including agricultural development; infrastructure improvement such as the upgrading of energy, telecommunications, and water and sanitation services; workforce development; education; and health.

[263] USAID, *Economic Growth and Trade* (2009), http://www.usaid.gov/our work/ economic growth and trade/.

[264] The 20 technical publications were selected from USAID's website on economic growth and trade.

[265] USAID, *A Guide to Economic Growth in Post-Conflict Countries* (January 2009), http://pdf.usaid.gov/pdf docs/PNADO408.pdf.

[266] USAID Armenia, *Country Profile*, http://armenia.usaid.gov/en/node/37.

[267] USAID interview, Armenia, *supra* note 231.

[268] USAID Ecuador, *Assistance to Persons with Disabilities*, http://ecuador.usaid.gov/portal /content/view/207/175/.

[269] *Id.*

[270] *Id.*

[271] *Id.*

[272] *Id.*

[273] *See* USAID, *Democracy and Governance User's Guide* (2010), http://www.usaid.gov/our work/democracy and governance/publications/pdfs/DG User Guide November10.pdf.

[274] USAID, *Rule of Law: Our Strategic Focus*, http://www.usaid.gov/our work/ democracyandg overnance/technicalareas/ruleoflaw/.

[275] *Id.*

[276] *Id.*

[277] *See* USAID, *Governance: Our Strategic Focus*, http://www.usaid.gov/our work/ democracy and governance/technical areas/governance/index.html.

[278] *See* USAID, *Governance: Our Strategic Goals and Programs*, http://www.usaid.gov/ our work/democracy and governance/technical areas/governance/gov strategy.html.

[279] *See* USAID, *Democracy and Governance: Technical Areas*, http://www.usaid.gov/our work/democracy and governance/technical areas/.

[280] *See* USAID, *Elections: Our Strategic Goals*, http://www.usaid.gov/ourwork/ democracy and governance/technical areas/elections/epp strategy.html.

[281] *See* USAID, *Civil Society: Strategic Focus*, http://www.usaid.gov/our work/ democracy and governance/technical areas/civil society/civ strategy.html.

[282] *See* USAID, *Civil Society*, http://www.usaid.gov/our work/democracy and governance/technical areas/dg office/civ.html.

[283] *See, for example*, USAID, *Rebuilding the Rule of Law in Post-Conflict Environments*; *Guide to Rule of Law Country Analysis: The Rule of Law Strategic Framework*; *Reducing Corruption in the Judiciary*; *Guidance for Promoting Judicial Independence and Impartiality*, *Case Tracking and Management Guide*; *Achievements in Building and Maintaining the Rule of Law*; *Alternative Dispute Resolution Practitioners' Guide*; *Weighing in on the Scales of Justice Independence and Impartiality*; *USAID Handbook on Legislative Strengthening*; *Understanding Representation: Legislative Strengthening*; *USAID Experience Strengthening Legislatures*.

[284] See USAID, *A Handbook on Fighting Corruption*; *Promoting Transparency and Accountability: USAID's Anti-Corruption Experience*; *USAID Anti-Corruption Strategy*.

[285] *See* USAID, *Policy Implementation: What USAID Has Learned*

[286] *See* USAID, *Money in Politics Handbook: A Guide to Increasing Transparency in Emerging Democracies Managing Assistance in Support of Political and Electoral*; *Electoral Security Framework*; *Political Party Assistance Policy*; *Political Party Development Assistance*.

[287] *See* USAID, *A Mobile Voice: The Use of Mobile Phones in Citizen Media*; *Community Media Sustainability Guide*; *New Media and International Media Development: A Resource Guide for Europe and Eurasia*; *The Enabling Environment for Free " Independent Media: Contribution to Transparent "Accountable Governance*; *Media Sustainability Index for Middle East and North Africa*; *The Role of Media in Democracy: A Strategic Approach*; *Approaches to Civic Education: Lessons Learned*; *Civil Society Groups and Political Parties: Supporting Constructive Relationships*; *Constituencies for Reform: Strategic Approaches for Donor-Supported Civic Advocacy*.

[288] USAID, *RFP International Rule of Law Technical Assistance Services*, SOL-OAA-11-000011 (December 7, 2010). "Support to ensure that laws are applied equally to all persons and entities, including women, youth, people with disabilities, the poor and disadvantaged, and other vulnerable populations, and that impunity of privileged individuals is reduced."

[289] USAID Liberia, RFA 669-11-001, Rule of Law.

[290] *Id.*

[291] *Id.*

[292] USAID Disability Policy, USAID Indonesia, APS-497-10-000001 "IKAT-US: Civil Societies Innovating Together."

[293] USAID interview, Vietnam, *supra* note 236.

[294] USAID Interview, Vietnam, *supra* note 236.

[295] USAID interview, Bangladesh, *supra* note 212.

[296] *See* DOS, "Mission," http://careers.state.gov/learn/what-we-do/mission.

[297] *See* DOS, "Bureau of Research Management," http://www.state.gov/s/d/rm/index.htm.

[298] *See* DOS, "Diplomacy: The U.S. Department of State at Work" (June 2008), at 1, http://www.state.gov/documents/organization/46839.pdf.

[299] *Id.*

[300] *See* DOS, "Conversations with America: International Disability Rights," http://www.state.gov/r/pa/plrmo/cwa/156916.htm.

[301] *Id.*

[302] *See* DOS, "Human Rights Reports," http://www.state.gov/g/drl/rls/hrrpt/.

[303] *Id.*

[304] *Id.*

[305] *See* DOS, "Human Rights," http://www.state.gov/g/drl/hr/index.htm.

[306] Examining the implications of the country human rights reports and other human rights documentation provided by DOS to the Immigration and Naturalization Service for asylum seekers is beyond the scope of this report. It stands to reason, however, that gaps in reporting on the human rights situation of marginalized populations is likely to have a chilling effect on successful asylum claims. Unfortunately, there is evidence to suggest that the lack of information on the human rights of people with disabilities is a barrier to successful asylum claims. *See, for example,* Arlene S. Kanter, Chisam, and Nugent, "The Right to Asylum and Need for Legal Representation of People with Mental Disabilities in Immigration Proceedings," 25 *Mental & Physical Disability L. Rep.* 511 (2001).

[307] NCD, Foreign Policy and Disability, *supra* note 50.

[308] *See* DOS, *2009 Human Rights Report: Israel and Occupied Territories* (March 11, 2010), http://www.state.gov/g/drl/rls/hrrpt/2009/nea/136070.htm.

[309] Although the territory is claimed by Morocco, Western Sahara's sovereignty is disputed. Presently, the country falls under Moroccan jurisdiction, and the Moroccan kingdom extends its laws, civil liberties, and restrictions to the Western Saharan population. The report's information about Western Sahara was obtained through the diplomatic mission to Morocco. It is also important to note that the United States does not have a diplomatic mission in Iran. All available information in the country report was gathered through nongovernmental sources.

[310] For instance, the Kazakhstan report states, "Violence against women, trafficking in persons, and discrimination against persons with disabilities, homosexual activity, and nonethnic Kazakhs in government were problems." DOS, *2009 Human Rights Report: Kazakhstan* (March 11, 2010), http://www.state.gov/g/drl/rls/hrrpt/2009/sca/136088.htm.

[311] *See* DOS, *2009 Human Rights Report: Romania* (March 11, 2010), http://www.state.gov/g/drl /rls/hrrpt/2009/eur/136053.htm.

[312] *See* DOS, *2009 Human Rights Report: Cameroon* (March 11, 2010), http://www.state.gov/g /drl/rls/hrrpt/2009/af/135942.htm

[313] *See* DOS, *2009 Human Rights Report: Kenya* (March 11, 2010), http://www.state.gov/g/drl /rls/hrrpt/2009/af/135959.htm

[314] *Id.*

[315] *See* DOS, *2009 Human Rights Report: Kosovo* (March 10, 2010), http://www.state.gov/g /drl/rls/hrrpt/2009/eur/136039.htm

[316] *See, e.g.,* DOS, *2009 Human Rights Report: Thailand* (March 10, 2010), http://www.state.gov /g/drl/rls/hrrpt/2009/eap/136010.htm.

[317] *See, e.g.,* DOS, *2009 Human Rights Report: India* (March 10, 2010), http://www.state.gov/g /drl/rls/hrrpt/2009/sca/136087.htm; *see also* DOS, *2009 Human Rights Report: Russia* (March 10, 2010), http://www.state.gov/g/drl/rls/hrrpt/2009/eur/136054.htm.

[318] It is not within the scope of this study to fully review the human rights situation of people with disabilities in each country; rather, this report aims to review whether and how DOS investigates and reports on such violations in country reports.

[319] *See* DOS, *2009 Human Rights Report: Ghana* (March 10, 2010), http://www.state.gov/g /drl/rls/hrrpt/2009/af/135956.htm

[320] *Id.*

[321] *Id.*

[322] *Id.*

[323] *See* DOS, *2009 Human Rights Report: Uganda* (March 10, 2010), http://www.state.gov/g /drl/rls/hrrpt/2009/af/135982.htm.

[324] *Id.*

[325] *Id.*

[326] *Id.*

[327] *See* DOS, *2009 Human Rights Report: Russia* (March 10, 2010), http://www.state.gov/g /drl/rls/hrrpt/2009/eur/136054.htm.

[328] *Id.*

[329] *Id.*

[330] *See* DOS, *2009 Human Rights Report: Armenia* (March 10,, 2010), http://www.state.gov /g/drl/rls/hrrpt/2009/eur/136018.htm.

[331] *Id.*

[332] *Id.*

[333] *Id.*

[334] *See* DOS, *2009 Human Rights Report: India*, http://www.state.gov/g/drl /rls/hrrpt/2009 /sca/136087.htm.

[335] *Id.*

[336] *See* DOS, *2009 Human Rights Report: Namibia*, http://www.state.gov/g/drl/rls /hrrpt/2009/af/135968.htm.

[337] *See* DOS, *2009 Human Rights Report: Zambia*, http://www.state.gov/g/drl/rls/hrrpt /2009/af/135983.htm.

[338] *Id.*

[339] *Id.*

[340] *See* DOS, *2009 Human Rights Report: Nepal*, http://www.state.gov/g/drl/rls/hrrpt /2009/sca/136091.htm.

[341] *Id.*

[342] *See* DOS, *2009 Human Rights Report: Colombia*, http://www.state.gov/g/drl/rls/hrrpt /2009/wha/136106.htm.

[343] *Id.*

[344] *Id.*

[345] Even where local disabled people's organizations are not readily identifiable to embassy personnel, one or two well-placed e-mails, either to the disability human rights advisor at DOS, the disability advisor at USAID, or to any number of international organizations working on disability rights (many of them in developing countries), would yield local DPO contact information.

[346] DOS, *2009 Human Rights Report: Mexico*, http://www.state.gov/g/drl/rls/hrrpt/ 2009/wha /136119.htm; DOS, *supra* note 337.

[347] QDDR, *supra* note 14.

[348] Twenty-two embassy websites were reviewed.

[349] Local advocate interview, U.S. embassy, Nepal.

[350] "About the Bureau [of Educational and Cultural Affairs]," http://exchanges.state. gov/about.html.

[351] *See* DOS, "History of the Bureau of Educational and Cultural Affairs," http://www.dipity.com /ecawebsitesmail/History-of-the-Bureau-of-Educational-andCultural-Affairs-U-S-Department-of-State/.

[352] *See* DOS, "About the Bureau," *supra* note 350.

[353] *Id.*

[354] *See* President's Committee on the Arts and Humanities, "Cultural Exchange," http://www. pcah.gov/cultural-exchange. *See also*, DOS, Bureau of Educational and Cultural Affairs [hereafter ECA], "About the Bureau," http://exchanges.state.gov/about.html.

[355] *See* DOS, "Exchange Visitors," http://travel.state.gov/visa/temp/types/ types1267.html#1.

[356] *See* DOS ECA, http://www.exchanges.state.gov/.

[357] *Id.*

[358] *See* DOS, "Fulbright," http://fulbright.state.gov/.

[359] MIUSA National Clearinghouse on Disability and Exchange, "Tools for Exchange Professionals," http://www.miusa.org/ncde/tools/index html.

[360] *Id.*

[361] *Id.*

[362] *Id.*

[363] *Id.*

[364] Council for International Exchange of Scholars, "Fulbright Specialist Program," http://www. cies.org/Webinar/2010/030310 Disabilities.pdf.

[365] "[N]o qualified disabled candidate will be subjected to discrimination on the basis of disability...." Mutual Education and Cultural Exchange Act of 1961, as amended, 22 U.S.C. § 2450 (2010).

[366] *Id.*

[367] *See* MIUSA, "U.S. State Department High School Exchange Programs: A-SMYLE, FLEX, & YES," http://www.miusa.org/exchange/flexyes.

[368] Stewart Patrick and Kaysie Brown, Center on Global Development, *The Pentagon and Global Development: Making Sense of the DoD's Expanding Role*, 3 (2007), http://www.cgdev.org /content/publications/detail/14815/.

[369] *Id.* at 1.

[370] *Id.* at 4.

[371] The Iraqi Relief and Reconstruction Fund was established by the U.S. Congress on November 6, 2003. It allocated $18.4 billion to rebuild Iraq's infrastructure, damaged from years of neglect, sanctions, and war. U.S. Department of Defense, *Iraq Rebuilding Shifts from Western Contracts to Iraqis* (2007), http://www.defense.gov/News/ NewsArticle.aspx?ID= 46592.

[372] The White House, *U.S. Support for Earthquake and Tsunami Victims* (January 3, 2005), http://georgewbush-whitehouse.archives.gov/infocus/tsunami/.

[373] Raymond W. Copson, Congressional Research Service, RS 21181, *HIV/AIDS International Programs: Appropriations, FY 2002–FY 2004* (2003), http://lugar.senate.gov/services /pdfcrs/foreign/AppropriationsHIVAIDS.pdf; Kaiser Family Foundation, HIV/AIDS Policy Fact Sheet, *U.S. Federal Funding for HIV AIDS: The President's FY 2011 Budget Request* (2010), http://www.kff.org/hivaids/upload/7029-06.pdf.

[374] OHDACA funds humanitarian programs that support humanitarian assistance (nonlethal excess property; medical visits; minor construction; repair of roads, schools, clinics; well digging; disaster preparedness); foreign disaster relief and emergency response (logistics, airlift, search and rescue, humanitarian daily rations, plastic sheeting, tents, water, capacity building); and humanitarian mine-related activities (the Humanitarian De-mining Training Center at Fort Leonard Wood, MO, funds deployments outside the Continental United States for de-mining and clearance training for other explosive remnants of war, mine risk education and awareness, medical, safety, organizational management). Defense Security Cooperation Agency, *Overseas Humanitarian, Disaster, and Civic Aid Appropriation*

(2011), http://comptroller.defense.gov/defbudget/fy2011/budget   justification/pdfs/01 Operation and Maintenance/O M VOL 1 PARTS/OHDACA FY11.pdf.

[375] AFRICOM is one of six DOD regional military headquarters and was declared a fully unified command on October 1, 2008. AFRICOM has administrative responsibility for U.S. military support to U.S. Government policy in Africa, to include military-to-military relationships with 53 African nations. The other five regional commands and their locations are U.S. Central Command, Tampa, Florida; U.S. European Command, Stuttgart, Germany; U.S. Northern Command, Colorado Springs, Colorado; U.S. Pacific Command, Honolulu, Hawaii; and U.S. Southern Command, Miami, Florida. U.S. Africa Command, http://www.africom.mil/.

[376] United States Access Board, *ABA Accessibility Standard for Department of Defense Facilities* (2008) [hereafter *ABA Accessibility Standard for DOD Facilities*], http://www.access-board.gov/ada-aba/aba-standards-dod.cfm.

[377] *Id.* at 101.1.

[378] Memorandum from deputy secretary of defense, "Dep't of Def, Access for People with Disabilities" (2008), http://www.access-board.gov/ada-aba/dod-memorandum.htm.

[379] *Id.*

[380] *Id.*

[381] *Id.*

[382] *ABA Accessibility Standard for DoD Facilities*, § F202.6 (1).

[383] USAID Sudan, *Strengthening Governance Project* (GOSS GOV Project), December 3, 2010, Draft Solicitation 650-11-002.

In: Accessibility and Inclusion of People ...   ISBN: 978-1-62808-324-8
Editor: Triston W. Pruett   © 2013 Nova Science Publishers, Inc.

Chapter 2

USAID DISABILITY POLICY PAPER*

U.S. Agency for International Development

I. USAID DISABILITY POLICY

The U.S. Agency for International Development (USAID) is committed to the inclusion of people who have physical and cognitive disabilities and those who advocate and offer services on behalf of people with disabilities. This commitment extends from the design and implementation of USAID programming to advocacy for and outreach to people with disabilities. USAID's policy on disability is as follows: To avoid discrimination against people with disabilities in programs which USAID funds and to stimulate an engagement of host country counterparts, governments, implementing organizations and other donors in promoting a climate of nondiscrimination against and equal opportunity for people with disabilities. The USAID policy on disability is to promote the inclusion of people with disabilities both within USAID programs and in host countries where USAID has programs.

For purposes of this policy, a disability is defined as a physical or cognitive impairment that affects a major life function, consistent with the definition of the Rehabilitation Act.

USAID commitment to disability issues is not new. A 1996 report ("Activities Addressing the Needs of Person with Disabilities," USAID

---

* This is an edited, reformatted and augmented version of the U.S. Agency for International Development publication, dated September 12, 1997.

document PN–ABY–746) described the many and varied Agency–sponsored activities in provisioning of prosthetics, treatment and prevention of blindness and special education, providing medical training of individuals who assist persons with disabilities, building advocacy and management capabilities of local organizations that represent the disabled, and the like. This policy is designed to build upon current activities and to enhance the effectiveness of the Agency's commitment.

The policy applies to Agency program funds only, and complements existing USAID disability policies which relate to staffing and personnel procedures. One of the best means of raising awareness in programs is to actively pursue those personnel procedures so that Agency staffing patterns reflect the intention of Agency programs.

The Americans with Disabilities Act of 1990 (ADA) is generally not applicable to USAID's overseas programs. While the ADA applies to U.S. citizens (including USAID employees) overseas, it does not apply to non–U.S. citizens, who are the primary beneficiaries of USAID programs. The USAID disability policy is thus in part an effort to extend the spirit of the ADA in areas beyond the jurisdiction of U.S. law.

II. POLICY OBJECTIVES

The objectives of the USAID policy on disability are: (a) to enhance the attainment of United States foreign assistance program goals by promoting the participation and equalization of opportunities of individuals with disabilities in USAID policy, country and sector strategies, activity designs and implementation; (b) to increase awareness of issues of people with disabilities both within USAID programs and in host countries; (c) to engage other U.S. government agencies, host country counterparts, governments, implementing organizations and other donors in fostering a climate of nondiscrimination against people with disabilities; and (d) to support international advocacy for people with disabilities.

III. POLICY FRAMEWORK

A substantial segment (often ten per cent or more) of any population has impairments. Those individuals are often limited in participating in society by obstacles in the physical or social environment. It is widely recognized that the response to this problem must be a balanced combination of prevention, rehabilitation and measures for the equalization of opportunities. Individuals with disabilities and their caregivers often are taken out of the workforce. The reasons are many: discrimination, lack of educational, vocational rehabilitation or training opportunities, etc. These factors place further economic burden on poor countries where USAID has sustainable development programs. People with disabilities have the same needs as others for nutrition, family planning, health care, training and employment. Many mainstream programs, with minor modification at the design stage, help address these needs. For example, education programs can be developed which promote inclusion of children with physical or cognitive disabilities to the maximum extent feasible. Economic growth activities, such as small business loans lending, can be developed to assure that people with disabilities have equal access to credit. Infrastructure projects can be designed, with acceptable marginal cost, to assure barrier—free access.

In providing humanitarian assistance in post—conflict situations and disaster assistance, early strategically aimed programs both help address the immediate needs of people with disabilities and also provide a foundation on which these individuals more effectively make a positive contribution to the economic development of their country. The disabling injuries caused by landmines provide yet another compelling reason for such programs.

USAID promotes advocacy as an integral part of its democracy and governance objective. As a world leader in the civil rights movement for people with disabilities, the U.S. has seen a strengthening of many local organizations which have formed to support independent living and other disability initiatives as a critical need. In many countries, individuals with disabilities have been 'warehoused' in abysmal conditions with total disrespect for their rights. Those rights must be respected. As young democracies decide where they will concentrate scarce resources, people with disabilities and those interested in the issues of people with disabilities must be among the voices that are heard.

Recently, in certain developing countries, indigenous non—governmental organizations (NGOs) interested in the concerns of people with disabilities have emerged. USAID's general policy with regard to partnership with private voluntary organizations (PVOs) encourages the use of U.S. PVOs to help strengthen indigenous NGOs ("USAID—U.S. PVO Partnership," April 12, 1995; Handbook 1, Policy Papers);

inclusion of NGOs interested in issues of persons with disabilities should be considered for this kind of support.

USAID also recognizes the appropriate role of host country governments in creating the enabling environment for disability advocacy and services. Host governments not only create the regulatory environment, but they also assure quality standards and, for donor programs, provide the basis for sustaining these efforts.[1]

IV. OPERATIONAL PROCEDURES

A. Consultation

Each USAID Bureau, Mission and Center of the Global Bureau must determine the best ways to consult with the disabled and with those who advocate on behalf of, or provide services for individuals with disabilities.

Each USAID Bureau, Mission and Center of the Global Bureau must also determine best ways for consulting with appropriate host government officials to assure that issues are reviewed with respect to the enabling environment, regulatory concerns, quality assurance standards and maintenance of donor–financed disability activities. USAID will also look to organizations and individuals with in–depth local experience to assist in designing and implementing participatory mechanisms to ensure that USAID strategic objectives and activities incorporate, to the extent feasible, the priorities and values of people with disabilities and groups pursuing these issues and interests in the host country.

B. Areas to Be Considered in the Consultative Process

The concerns of people with physical and cognitive disabilities should be considered in the variety of USAID programs for the poorest elements of society including but not limited to programs for children and women, especially early childhood interventions, child survival programs and curriculum development for special education within basic education programs; mass communication and printed materials; development of basic infrastructure (e.g., roads, water and sanitation, public transportation, telecommunications); development of small scale industries or workshops; introduction of new machinery; development of products the use of which requires specific skills; urban or rural community development; development of health care facilities or systems; development of formal and non–formal education, training, career development and job placement services; family planning and health education programs; design and construction activities; and activities related to democracy and good governance, human rights initiatives, and income generation. Where appropriate, USAID may also encourage relevant policy dialogue with host governments.

C. Supporting U.S. PVO and Indigenous NGO Relationships

Indigenous NGOs, as part of the host society, can serve as a voice for the interests and perspectives of the community of individuals with disabilities or groups interested in their issues. USAID will look to an increasing role for indigenous NGOs to carry out service delivery and to advocate on behalf of the interests of people with disabilities. USAID will actively encourage the formation of effective partnership relations between U.S. PVOs and indigenous NGOs interested in issues of concern to people with disabilities.

D. Training and Enhanced Awareness

USAID employees and contractors will be trained in issues of relevance to people with disabilities so that, as appropriate, USAID programs reflect those issues. Grantees and contractors will be encouraged to provide relevant training to their staff.

USAID DISABILITY PLAN OF ACTION "MANDATORY REFERENCE" AUGUST, 1997

This Plan of Action is designed to direct the implementation of USAID's Disability Policy. It does so by outlining ways to promote the inclusion of services with and for persons with disabilities in programs throughout the Agency. The Plan of Action is applicable to Agency program activities only, and is consistent with chapters in Series 200 of the Agency's Automated Directive System that deal with personnel and staffing issues (http://www.

usaid.gov/M/HR/ads1/htm). The Plan of Action does not require additional personnel, financial reporting, or other elaborate reporting systems. It is designed to be used within existing level of resources, and to complement reengineering guidelines.

1.In order to finalize the establishment of Agency policy on persons with disabilities, the following process will be pursued:

- The draft policy shall be reviewed by field missions, development partners, and other donors. (Action: Policy and Program Coordination Bureau (PPC), completed)
- The policy shall be revised and submitted for the approval of the Administrator. (Action: PPC, summer '97)

2. In order to encourage interagency donor collaboration on the issues of inclusion of disability issues in international programming, USAID will participate actively in relevant interagency and inter–donor meetings.

- USAID participated in the first interagency donor meeting on disabilities held at the World Bank. Also in attendance were representatives from the United Nations' Office of Disabled Persons, the World Health Organization (WHO), the United Nations Children's Fund (UNICEF), the United Nations' Educational, Scientific and Cultural Organization (UNESCO), the Inter–American Development Bank, the Danish International Development Assistance organization (DANIDA), the Organization for Economic Cooperation and Development's Center for Educational Research and Innovation, the African Development Foundation, the U.S. Department of Health and Human Services, the Academy for Educational Development and several international disabilities NGOs. (Action: Global Bureau, completed)
- USAID will participate in quarterly meetings of this interagency working group, and will chair the second interagency meeting. USAID will contribute to setting the mission statement, objectives and activities of this group. (Action: Global Bureau, pending appointment of the Team Coordinator; see 4 below)
- USAID will explore the development of an international working group with other federal agencies that have programs serving persons with disabilities, e.g. Department of State, U.S. Information Agency, the National Council on Disability, Department of Treasury,

Department of Commerce, Department of Education, Department of Health and Human Services including the National Institutes of Health, the President's Committee on Employment of People with Disabilities, Department of Housing and Urban Development, Social Security Administration, Department of Justice, Department of Transportation, the Access Board, etc. (Action: Team Coordinator, Oct 1, '97)

3. In order to ensure Agency—wide coordination and responsiveness, and to assist and facilitate consideration of disability issues in field and Washington planning, an Agency Team for Disability Programming (ATDP) will be established. Membership will be by invitation of the Administrator, and may include external representatives. No budgetary resources will be required.

- The ATDP will meet quarterly under the leadership of PPC. (Action: The Administrator and USAID/PPC, beginning Sept 30, '97)
- The ATDP will consult annually with various international disabilities organizations, the PVO community through USAID's Advisory Committee on Voluntary Foreign Assistance (ACVFA), the higher education community through the Association Liaison Office for University Cooperation in Development (ALO), and with other organizations and donors through the quarterly interagency donor collaboration meetings (mentioned above). (Action: Team Coordinator, '97)
- The ATDP will foster Agency awareness (e.g. Agency newsletters, USAID Focus, USAID/PPC's Center for Development Information and Evaluation (CDIE) publications, ExoNet, Agency home page, etc.) regarding the importance of including persons with disabilities in USAID programs; promote Agency commitment and responsiveness; and ensure bureau, mission and center review processes occur. (see number 5 below). (Action: ATDP, CDIE, and Public Affairs Bureau, continuous)
- The ATDP will review [or develop] activity reports, identify "lessons learned", and assess the Agency's training program (see point 6 below). A summary annual [or periodic] review will be presented to the Administrator. (Action: ATDP, quarterly)
- The ATDP may establish short—term special working groups, when needed. (Action: ATDP, as needed)

- The ATDP may consider and recommend the establishment of special Agency–wide activities focused on policy and services for persons with disabilities. (Action: ATDP, as needed)
- The ATDP will provide senior staff with an annual briefing on all disability–related activities. (Action: ATDP, each January)
- An Annual Disabilities Recognition Award will be established to recognize USAID staff and/or partners who have promoted integration of disabilities awareness and activities into USAID programs. The ATDP will make information about the Award widely available, identify potential recipients, and provide the Administrator with recommendations for candidates. (Action: ATDP, each June 30)

4. In order to ensure that a central team leader and contact point for activities regarding persons with disabilities exists within the Agency, the Administrator will designate a Disability Team Coordinator.

- This Team Coordinator will provide support to the ATDP upon request, provide technical assistance to all bureaus, missions and centers as they assess their programs for opportunities to include persons with disabilities, maintain the flow of information on disabilities activities, respond to external enquiries, represent USAID at conferences and meetings on disability or ensure proper representation for technical matters, alert NGOs, institutions of higher education and other organizations about "windows of opportunity" in USAID programs, attend and brief participants at regional bureau conferences and other large–scale Agency meetings, and liaise with disabilities organizations, ACVFA, ALO and key U.S. PVO/NGOs involved with disabilities programming.(Action: USAID Administrator, Oct 1, '97)

5. In order to address appropriately and fully the inclusion of persons with disabilities in Agency programs, the Agency will track progress by compiling an annual [or periodic] summary report.

USAID/Washington will periodically compile a report that assesses the extent and quality of USAID disability activities, and identifies lessons learned, new models, opportunities and challenges for future programming. Relevant field programs may be visited. The first summary report will be sent to the Administrator with, as needed, recommendations for ensuring Agency momentum and progress on disabilities issues. (Action: ATDP, first report to be completed July 1998.)

6. In order to promote inclusion and build commitment and capacity to address issues regarding persons with disabilities, the Agency will conduct staff development activities.

- Appropriate training materials for Agency staff members, contractors and other partners will be designed or adapted, field tested and produced, including items such as: a video with practical examples of programs that work; handouts for reflection and action; discussion frameworks for group activities; and suggestions regarding policy implementation. (Action: Team Coordinator and Training Office, for use beginning March 30, 1998)
- Preliminary staff training will be provided within new employee orientation, diversity training, other relevant on-going staff training sessions and special technical training, as feasible. Operating units will be encouraged to engage in follow-on self-training through the use of the training materials. (Action: Training Office and operating units, beginning as soon as feasible)
- A letter with abbreviated training materials will be distributed to all Agency contractors, grantees and cooperative agreement partners to encourage them to engage in staff training regarding programming for persons with disabilities. Such organizations will also be encouraged to share their relevant training materials with USAID for review and possible use in our training activities. (Action: Training and Procurement Offices, beginning October 1, 1997)

POLICY PAPER

USAID/General Notice
PPC
09/12/97

This policy paper articulates the U.S. Agency for International Development's (USAID) commitment to pursue advocacy for, outreach to, and inclusion of people with physical and cognitive disabilities, to the maximum extent feasible, in the design and implementation of USAID programming, and provides guidance for making that commitment operational.

It is the product of a comprehensive consultative process between USAID and its partners, and responds to issues identified in that process. Note that this policy applies to the use of Agency program funds only and complements USAID's personnel and staffing disability policies. The paper provides the basis from which a policy directive will be developed.

This policy paper does not represent a new initiative. Instead it describes the importance of considering concerns of the disabled within ongoing and future programs. Implementation of the policy will be within existing staff and financial resource levels as determined by each operating unit, and no additional financial reporting will be necessary.

The paper outlines the fundamental principles on which the USAID disability policy is based, including: (1) need for a comprehensive and consistent approach to considering people with disabilities, being sure to include women and children, within USAID and in USAID assisted activities; (2) outreach to and early consultation with persons with disabilities and the community of organizations concerned about them as part of ongoing participatory processes; (3) intent to work as development partners with US and foreign PVOs and NGOs committed to persons with disabilities and to facilitate relationships among these entities; and (4) encouragement of U.S. interagency collaboration and networking among donors and other diverse entities concerned about persons with disabilities with a view to increasing impact and sustaining these efforts.

End Note

[1] The National Council on Disability (NCD) is an independent federal agency which was established to promote policies, programs, practices and procedures that guarantee equal opportunity for all individuals with disabilities and to empower individuals with disabilities to achieve economic self– sufficiency, independent living, and inclusion and integration into all aspects of society, and to provide an annual report to the President and the Congress. The NCD issued a report on August 1, 1996, entitled, "Foreign Policy and Disability" which asked whether the United States maintains a coherent disability policy within its foreign policy and found in the negative. In fact, the report concluded that "those responsible for creating and implementing U.S. overseas policies and programs generally lack awareness of disability issues, cannot articulate our national policies with respect to people with disabilities, do not incorporate the interests of people with disabilities into U.S. foreign policy objectives, and do not see the importance of U.S. disability advances and achievements for people with disabilities in other countries." The NCD recommended:

- creating a comprehensive foreign policy on disability to advocate for people with disabilities through activities on international levels;

- extending U.S. disability law by legislation or executive order to include unambiguously the international operations of the U.S. government;
- employing domestic standards of nondiscrimination in U.S.–sponsored international activities;
- training U.S. foreign affairs agencies and their contractors to plan for programmatic accessibility; and,
- establishing the principle that no U.S. international activity should have a lower standard of inclusion than its domestic correlate.

Bureau for Policy and Program Coordination (PPC)
U.S. Agency for International Development
Washington, D.C. 20523
September 12, 1997

POINT OF CONTACT FOR THIS NOTICE IS PPC, HIRAM LAREW, (202) 647–7065.

INDEX

F

G

H

S